Distributed Computing with Python

Harness the power of multiple computers using Python through this fast-paced informative guide

Francesco Pierfederici

PUBLISHING

BIRMINGHAM - MUMBAI

Distributed Computing with Python

First published: April 2016

Production reference: 1060416

Published by Packt Publishing Ltd.
Livery Place
35 Livery Street
Birmingham B3 2PB, UK.

ISBN 978-1-78588-969-1

www.packtpub.com

Credits

Author
Francesco Pierfederici

Reviewer
James King

Commissioning Editor
Veena Pagare

Acquisition Editor
Aaron Lazar

Content Development Editor
Parshva Sheth

Technical Editor
Abhishek R. Kotian

Copy Editor
Neha Vyas

Project Coordinator
Nikhil Nair

Proofreader
Safis Editing

Indexer
Rekha Nair

Graphics
Disha Haria

Production Coordinator
Melwyn Dsa

Cover Work
Melwyn Dsa

About the Author

Francesco Pierfederici is a software engineer who loves Python. He has been working in the fields of astronomy, biology, and numerical weather forecasting for the last 20 years.

He has built large distributed systems that make use of tens of thousands of cores at a time and run on some of the fastest supercomputers in the world. He has also written a lot of applications of dubious usefulness but that are great fun. Mostly, he just likes to build things.

I would like to thank my wife, Alicia, for her unreasonable patience during the gestation of this book. I would also like to thank Parshva Sheth and Aaron Lazar at Packt Publishing and the technical reviewer, James King, who were all instrumental in making this a better book.

About the Reviewer

James King is a software developer with a broad range of experience in distributed systems. He is a contributor to many open source projects including OpenStack and Mozilla Firefox. He enjoys mathematics, horsing around with his kids, games, and art.

www.PacktPub.com

eBooks, discount offers, and more

Did you know that Packt offers eBook versions of every book published, with PDF and ePub files available? You can upgrade to the eBook version at www.PacktPub.com and as a print book customer, you are entitled to a discount on the eBook copy. Get in touch with us at customercare@packtpub.com for more details.

At www.PacktPub.com, you can also read a collection of free technical articles, sign up for a range of free newsletters and receive exclusive discounts and offers on Packt books and eBooks.

https://www2.packtpub.com/books/subscription/packtlib

Do you need instant solutions to your IT questions? PacktLib is Packt's online digital book library. Here, you can search, access, and read Packt's entire library of books.

Why subscribe?

- Fully searchable across every book published by Packt
- Copy and paste, print, and bookmark content
- On demand and accessible via a web browser

Table of Contents

Preface

Parallel and distributed computing is a fascinating subject that only a few years ago developers in only a very few large companies and national labs were privy to. Things have changed dramatically in the last decade or so, and now everybody can build small- and medium-scale distributed applications in a variety of programming languages including, of course, our favorite one: Python.

This book is a very practical guide for Python programmers who are starting to build their own distributed systems. It starts off by illustrating the bare minimum theoretical concepts needed to understand parallel and distributed computing in order to lay the basic foundations required for the rest of the (more practical) chapters.

It then looks at some first examples of parallelism using nothing more than modules from the Python standard library. The next step is to move beyond the confines of a single computer and start using more and more nodes. This is accomplished using a number of third-party libraries, including Celery and Pyro.

The remaining chapters investigate a few deployment options for our distributed applications. The cloud and classic High Performance Computing (HPC) clusters, together with their strengths and challenges, take center stage.

Finally, the thorny issues of monitoring, logging, profiling, and debugging are touched upon.

All in all, this is very much a hands-on book, teaching you how to use some of the most common frameworks and methodologies to build parallel and distributed systems in Python.

What this book covers

Chapter 1, An Introduction to Parallel and Distributed Computing, takes you through the basic theoretical foundations of parallel and distributed computing.

Chapter 2, Asynchronous Programming, describes the two main programming styles used in distributed applications: synchronous and asynchronous programming.

Chapter 3, Parallelism in Python, shows you how to do more than one thing at the same time in your Python code, using nothing more than the Python standard library.

Chapter 4, Distributed Applications – with Celery, teaches you how to build simple distributed applications using Celery and some of its competitors: Python-RQ and Pyro.

Chapter 5, Python in the Cloud, shows how you can deploy your Python applications on the cloud using Amazon Web Services.

Chapter 6, Python on an HPC Cluster, shows how to deploy your Python applications on a classic HPC cluster, typical of many universities and national labs.

Chapter 7, Testing and Debugging Distributed Applications, talks about the challenges of testing, profiling, and debugging distributed applications in Python.

Chapter 8, The Road Ahead, looks at what you have learned so far and which directions interested readers could take to push their development of distributed systems further.

What you need for this book

The following software and hardware is recommended:

- Python 3.5 or later
- A laptop or desktop computer running Linux or Mac OS X
- Ideally, some extra computers or some extra virtual machines to test your distributed applications

All software mentioned in this book is free of charge and can be downloaded from the Internet with the exception of PBS Pro, which is commercial. Most of the PBS Pro functionality, however, is available in its close sibling Torque, which is open source.

Who this book is for

This book is for developers who already know Python and want to learn how to parallelize their code and/or write distributed systems. While a Unix environment is assumed, most if not all of the examples should also work on Windows systems.

Conventions

In this book, you will find a number of text styles that distinguish between different kinds of information. Here are some examples of these styles and an explanation of their meaning.

Code words in text, database table names, folder names, filenames, file extensions, pathnames, dummy URLs, user input, and Twitter handles are shown as follows: "Import the `concurrent.futures` module."

A block of code is set as follows:

```
class Foo:
    def __init__(self):
        """Docstring"""
        self.bar = 42
        # A comment
        return
```

Any command-line input or output is written as follows:

```
bookuser@hostname$ python3.5 ./foo.py
```

New terms and **important words** are shown in bold. Words that you see on the screen, for example, in menus or dialog boxes, appear in the text like this: "Clicking the **Next** button moves you to the next screen."

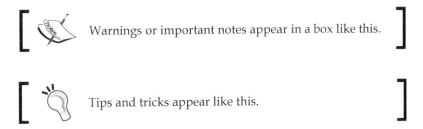

> Warnings or important notes appear in a box like this.

> Tips and tricks appear like this.

Reader feedback

Feedback from our readers is always welcome. Let us know what you think about this book—what you liked or disliked. Reader feedback is important for us as it helps us develop titles that you will really get the most out of.

To send us general feedback, simply e-mail feedback@packtpub.com, and mention the book's title in the subject of your message.

If there is a topic that you have expertise in and you are interested in either writing or contributing to a book, see our author guide at www.packtpub.com/authors.

Customer support

Now that you are the proud owner of a Packt book, we have a number of things to help you to get the most from your purchase.

Downloading the example code

You can download the example code files for this book from your account at http://www.packtpub.com. If you purchased this book elsewhere, you can visit http://www.packtpub.com/support and register to have the files e-mailed directly to you.

You can download the code files by following these steps:

1. Log in or register to our website using your e-mail address and password.
2. Hover the mouse pointer on the **SUPPORT** tab at the top.
3. Click on **Code Downloads & Errata**.
4. Enter the name of the book in the **Search** box.
5. Select the book for which you're looking to download the code files.
6. Choose from the drop-down menu where you purchased this book from.
7. Click on **Code Download**.

Once the file is downloaded, please make sure that you unzip or extract the folder using the latest version of:

- WinRAR / 7-Zip for Windows
- Zipeg / iZip / UnRarX for Mac
- 7-Zip / PeaZip for Linux

Errata

Although we have taken every care to ensure the accuracy of our content, mistakes do happen. If you find a mistake in one of our books—maybe a mistake in the text or the code—we would be grateful if you could report this to us. By doing so, you can save other readers from frustration and help us improve subsequent versions of this book. If you find any errata, please report them by visiting http://www.packtpub. com/submit-errata, selecting your book, clicking on the **Errata Submission Form** link, and entering the details of your errata. Once your errata are verified, your submission will be accepted and the errata will be uploaded to our website or added to any list of existing errata under the Errata section of that title.

To view the previously submitted errata, go to https://www.packtpub.com/books/ content/support and enter the name of the book in the search field. The required information will appear under the **Errata** section.

Piracy

Piracy of copyrighted material on the Internet is an ongoing problem across all media. At Packt, we take the protection of our copyright and licenses very seriously. If you come across any illegal copies of our works in any form on the Internet, please provide us with the location address or website name immediately so that we can pursue a remedy.

Please contact us at copyright@packtpub.com with a link to the suspected pirated material.

We appreciate your help in protecting our authors and our ability to bring you valuable content.

Questions

If you have a problem with any aspect of this book, you can contact us at questions@packtpub.com, and we will do our best to address the problem.

1

An Introduction to Parallel and Distributed Computing

The first modern digital computer was invented in the late 30s and early 40s (that is, arguably, the **Z1** from Konrad Zuse in 1936), probably before most of the readers of this book — let alone the author — were born. These last seventy odd years have seen computers become faster and cheaper at an amazing rate, which was unique across industries. Just think that today's smartphones (for example, the latest iPhones or Android phones) are faster than the fastest computer in the world from just 20 years ago. Not to mention, the amazing feat of miniaturization: those supercomputers used to take up entire rooms; now they fit in our pockets.

These years have also seen, among others, two key inventions relevant to the topic at hand. One is the ability to cram more than one processor on a single motherboard (and even multiple CPU cores on a single processor). This development was crucial in allowing computations to be performed truly concurrently. As we know, processors are able to perform only one task at a time; however, as we will see later on in the chapter, they are fast enough to give the illusion of being able to run multiple tasks at the same time. To be able to perform more than one action exactly at the same time, you need access to more than one processor.

The other critical invention is high-speed computer networking. This allowed, for the first time, a potentially enormous number of computers to communicate with each other. These networked machines can either be located in the same office/building (the so-called **Local Area Network (LAN)**) or be spread out across different buildings, cities, or even across the planet (that is, WAN or wide area networking).

By now, most of us are familiar with multiprocessor/multicore computers, and indeed, the chances are pretty high that the phone in our pocket, the tablet in our hands, or the laptop we take on the road has a handful of cores already. The graphics card, also called **Graphics Processing Unit (GPU)** in these devices is more often than not massively parallel, with hundreds or even thousands of processing units. Computer networks too are all around us, starting from the most famous of them all: the Internet, to the Wi-Fi in our homes and coffee shops and the 4G mobile networks our phones use.

In the rest of this chapter, we will lay some working definitions of the topics that we will explore in the rest of the book. We will be introducing the concepts of parallel and distributed computing. We will give some examples of each that are taken from familiar topics and technologies. Some general advantages and disadvantages of each architecture and programming paradigm will be discussed as well.

Before proceeding with our definitions and a little bit of theory, let's clarify a possible source of confusion. In this and the following chapters, we will use the term **processor** and the term **CPU core** (or even simply **core**) interchangeably, unless otherwise specified. This is, of course, technically incorrect; a processor has one or more cores, and a computer has one or more processors as cores do not exist in isolation. Depending on the algorithm and its performance requirements, running on multiple processors or on a single processor using multiple cores can make a bit of difference in speed, assuming, of course, that the algorithm can be parallelized in the first place. For our intents and purposes, however, we will ignore these differences and refer to more advanced texts for further exploration of this topic.

Parallel computing

Definitions of parallel computing abound. However, for the purpose of this book, a simple definition will suffice, which is as follows:

> *Parallel computing is the simultaneous use of more than one processor to solve a problem.*

Typically, this definition is further specialized by requiring that the processors reside on the same motherboard. This is mostly to distinguish parallel computing from distributed computing (which is discussed in the next section).

The idea of splitting work among many workers is as old as human civilization, is not restricted to the digital world, and finds an immediate and obvious application in modern computers equipped with higher and higher numbers of compute units.

There are, of course, many reasons why parallel computing might be useful and even necessary. The simplest one is performance; if we can indeed break up a long-running computation into smaller chunks and parcel them out to different processors, then we can do more work in the same amount of time.

Other times, and just as often, parallel computing techniques are used to present users with responsive interfaces while the system is busy with some other task. Remember that one processor executes just one task at the time. Applications with GUIs need to offload work to a separate thread of execution running on another processor so that one processor is free to update the GUI and respond to user inputs.

The following figure illustrates this common architecture, where the main thread is processing user and system inputs using what is called an **event loop**. Tasks that require a long time to execute and those that would otherwise block the GUI are offloaded to a background or worker thread:

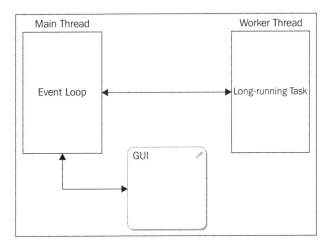

A simple real-world example of this parallel architecture could be a photo organization application. When we connect a digital camera or a smartphone to our computers, the photo application needs to perform a number of actions; all the while its user interface needs to stay interactive. For instance, our application needs to copy images from the device to the internal disk, create thumbnails, extract metadata (for example, date and time of the shot), index the images, and finally update the image gallery. While all of this happens, we are still able to browse images that are already imported, open them, edit them, and so on.

Of course, all these actions could very well be performed sequentially on a single processor—the same processor that is handling the GUI. The drawback would be a sluggish interface and an extremely slow overall application. Performing these steps in parallel keeps the application snappy and its users happy.

The astute reader might jump up at this point and rightfully point out that older computers, with a single processor and a single core, could already perform multiple things *at the same time* (by way of multitasking). What happened back then (and even today, when we launch more tasks than there are processors and cores on our computers) was that the one running task gave up the CPU (either voluntarily or forcibly by the OS, for example, in response to an IO event) so that another task could run in its place. These interrupts would happen over and over again, with various tasks acquiring and giving up the CPU many times over the course of the application's life. In those cases, users had the impression of multiple tasks running concurrently, as the switches were extremely fast. In reality, however, only one task was running at any given time.

The typical tools used in parallel applications are threads. On systems such as Python (as we will see in *Chapter 3, Parallelism in Python*) where threads have significant limitations, programmers resort to launching (oftentimes, by means of forking) subprocesses instead. These subprocesses replace (or complement) threads and run alongside the main application process.

The first technique is called **multithreaded programming**. The second is called **multiprocessing**. It is worth noting that multiprocessing should not be seen as inferior or as a workaround with respect to using multiple threads.

There are many situations where multiprocessing is preferable to multiple threads. Interestingly, even though they both run on a single computer, a multithreaded application is an example of shared-memory architecture, whereas a multiprocess application is an example of distributed memory architecture (refer to the following section to know more).

Distributed computing

For the remainder of this book, we will adopt the following working definition of distributed computing:

> *Distributed computing is the simultaneous use of more than one computer to solve a problem.*

Typically, as in the case of parallel computing, this definition is oftentimes further restricted. The restriction usually is the requirement that these computers appear to their users as a single machine, therefore hiding the distributed nature of the application. In this book, we will be happy with the more general definition.

Distributing computation across multiple computers is again a pretty obvious strategy when using systems that are able to speak to each other over the (local or otherwise) network. In many respects, in fact, this is just a generalization of the concepts of parallel computing that we saw in the previous section.

Reasons to build distributed systems abound. Oftentimes, the reason is the ability to tackle a problem so big that no individual computer could handle it at all, or at least, not in a reasonable amount of time. An interesting example from a field that is probably familiar to most of us is the rendering of 3D animation movies, such as those from Pixar and DreamWorks.

Given the sheer number of frames to render for a full-length feature (30 frames per second on a two-hour movie is a lot!), movie studios need to spread the full-rendering job to large numbers of computers (**computer farms** as they are called).

Other times, the very nature of the application being developed requires a distributed system. This is the case, for instance, for instant messaging and video conferencing applications. For these pieces of software, performance is not the main driver. It is just that the problem that the application solves is itself distributed.

In the following figure, we see a very common web application architecture (another example of a distributed application), where multiple users connect to the website over the network. At the same time, the application itself communicates with systems (such as a database server) running on different machines in its LAN:

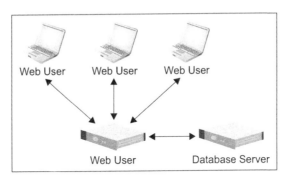

Another interesting example of distributed systems, which might be a bit counterintuitive, is the CPU-GPU combination. These days, graphics cards are very sophisticated computers in their own right. They are highly parallel and offer compelling performance for a large number of compute-intensive problems, not just for displaying images on screen. Tools and libraries exist to allow programmers to make use of GPUs for general-purpose computing (for example **CUDA** from NVIDIA, **OpenCL**, and **OpenAcc** among others).

However, the system composed by the CPU and GPU is really an example of a distributed system, where the network is replaced by the PCI bus. Any application exploiting both the CPU and the GPU needs to take care of data movement between the two subsystems just like a more traditional application running across the network!

It is worth noting that, in general, adapting the existing code to run across computers on a network (or on the GPU) is far from a simple exercise. In these cases, I find it quite helpful to go through the intermediate step of using multiple processes on a single computer first (refer to the discussion in the previous section). Python, as we will see in *Chapter 3, Parallelism in Python*, has powerful facilities for doing just that (refer to the `concurrent.futures` module).

Once I evolve my application so that it uses multiple processes to perform operations in parallel, I start thinking about how to turn these processes into separate applications altogether, which are no longer part of my monolithic core.

Special attention must be given to the data—where to store it and how to access it. In simple cases, a shared filesystem (for example, NFS on Unix systems) is enough; other times, a database and/or a message bus is needed. We will see some concrete examples from *Chapter 4, Distributed Applications – with Celery*, onwards. It is important to remember that, more often than not, data, rather than CPU, is the real bottleneck.

Shared memory versus distributed memory

Conceptually, parallel computing and distributed computing look very similar—after all, they both are about breaking up some computation into several smaller parts and running those on processors. Some of you might ponder upon the fact that in one case the processors in use are part of the same computer, whereas in the other case they are physically on different computers; is this just a trivial technicality?

The answer is maybe. As we saw, some applications are fundamentally distributed. Others simply need more performance than they can get on a single box. For some of these applications, the answer is maybe yes—it does not really matter where the processing power comes from. However, in all cases, the physical location of the hardware resources in use has significant implications.

Possibly, the most obvious difference between parallel and distributed computing is in the underlying memory architecture and access patterns. In the case of a parallel application, all concurrent tasks can—in principle—access the same memory space. Here, we have to say *in principle* because as we have already saw, parallelism does not necessary imply the use of threads (which can indeed access the same memory space).

In the following figure, we see a typical shared-memory architecture where four processors (the four CPU boxes in the following diagram) can all access the same memory address space (that is, the Memory box). If our application were to use threads, then those would be able to access exactly the same memory locations, if needed:

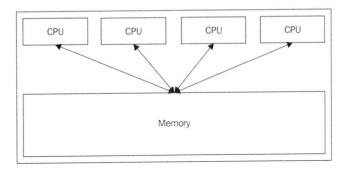

In the case of a distributed application, however, the various concurrent tasks cannot normally access the same memory space. The reason being that some tasks run on one computer and others on another, physically separated, computer.

Since these computers are able to talk to each other over the network, one could imagine writing a software layer (a middleware) that could present our application with a unified logical (as opposed to physical) memory space. These types of middlewares do exist and implement what is known as distributed shared-memory architecture. We will not examine these systems in this book.

In the following figure, we have the same four CPUs as before, that are organized now in a shared-memory architecture. Each CPU has access to its own private memory and cannot see any other CPU memory space. The four computers (indicated by the boxes surrounding their CPU and memory) communicate through the network (the black line connecting them). Each data transfer between boxes happens over the network:

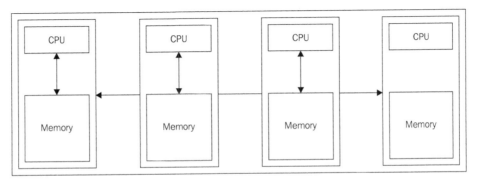

In reality, the computers one is likely to use nowadays are a hybrid of the two extremes that we just described in the previous section. Computers communicate over the network just like in a pure distributed-memory architecture. However, each computer has more than one processor and/or processor core, implementing a shared-memory architecture. The following figure schematically illustrates such a hybrid architecture that is shared within each individual computer (indicated by a box enclosing two CPUs and its own memory) and distributed across boxes (linked together via the network):

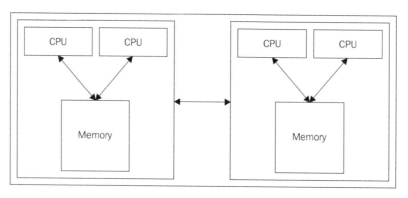

Each of these architectures has its own pros and cons. In the case of shared-memory systems, sharing data across various concurrent threads of a single executable is quite fast and tremendously faster than using the network. In addition, having a single, uniform memory address space makes writing the code arguably simpler.

At the same time, special care has to be exercised in the design of the program to avoid multiple threads from stepping on each other's toes and changing variables *behind each other's backs*.

A distributed memory system tends to be very scalable and cheap to assemble; need more power? Simply add another box. Another advantage is that processors can access their own memory in isolation without worrying about race conditions (while this is technically true, oftentimes, different tasks running in parallel need to read and write data in a common repository, for example, a database or a shared filesystem. In those cases, we still have to deal with race conditions). Disadvantages of this system include the fact that programmers need to implement their own strategy to move data around and they need to worry about issues of data locality. Also, not all algorithms easily map to these architectures.

Amdahl's law

The last important concept of this chapter is a behavior known as **Amdahl's law**. In simple terms, Amdahl's law states that we can parallelize/distribute our computations as much as we want, gaining in performance as we add compute resources. However, our code cannot be faster than the speed of its combined sequential (that is, non parallelizable) parts on a single processor.

Put more formally, Amdahl's law has the following formulation. Given an algorithm that is partially parallel, let's call P its parallel fraction and S its serial (that is, non parallel) fraction (clearly, $S+P=100\%$). Furthermore, let's call $T(n)$ the runtime (in seconds) of the algorithm when using n processors. Then, the following relation holds:

$$T(n) \geq S * T(1) + \frac{P * T(1)}{n}$$

The preceding relation, translated in plain English states the following:

The execution time of the algorithm described here on n processors is equal—and generally greater—than the execution time of its serial part on one processor (that is, $S*T(1)$) plus the execution time of its parallel part on one processor (that is, $P*T(1)$) divided by n: the number of processors.

As we increase the number, n, of processors used by our code, the second term on the equation becomes smaller and smaller, eventually becoming negligible with respect to the first term. In those cases, the preceding relation simply becomes this:

$$T(\infty) \approx S * T(1)$$

The translation of this relation in plain English is as follows:

The execution time of the algorithm described here on an infinite number of processors (that is, a really large number of processors) is approximately equal to the execution time of its serial part on a single processor (that is, $S*T(1)$).

Now, let's stop for a second and think about the implication of Amdahl's law. What we have here is a pretty simple observation: oftentimes, we cannot fully parallelize our algorithms.

Which means that, most of the time, we cannot have *S=0* in the preceding relations. The reasons for this are numerous: we might have to copy data and/or code to where the various processors will be able to access them. We might have to split the data into chunks and move those chunks over the network. We might have to collect the results of all the concurrent tasks and perform some further processing on them, and so on.

Whatever the reason, if we cannot fully parallelize our algorithm, eventually the runtime of our code will be dominated by the performance of the serial fraction. Not only that, but even before that happens, we will start to see increasingly worse-than-expected speedups.

As a side note, algorithms that are fully parallel are usually called **embarrassingly parallel** or, in a more politically correct way, pleasantly parallel and offer impressive scalability properties (with speedups often linear with the number of processors). Of course, there is nothing embarrassing about those pieces of software! Unfortunately, they are not as common as we would like.

Let's try to visualize the entire Amdahl's law with some numbers. Assume that our algorithm takes 100 seconds on a single processor. Let's also assume that we can parallelize 99% of it, which would be a pretty amazing feat, most of the time. We can make our code go faster by increasing the number of processor we use, as expected. Let's take at look at the following calculation:

$$T(1) = 100s$$

$$T(10) \approx 0.01 * 100s + \frac{0.99 * 100s}{10} = 10.9s \Rightarrow 9.2X \; speedup$$

$$T(100) \approx 1s + 0.99s = 1.99s \Rightarrow 50.2X \; speedup$$

$$T(1000) \approx 1s + 0.099s = 1.099s \Rightarrow 91X \; speedup$$

We can see from the preceding numbers that the speedup increase with increasing values of *n* is rather disappointing. We start with a truly amazing *9.2X* speedup using 10 processors, and then we drop to just *50X* when using 100 processors and a paltry *91X* when using 1,000 processors!

The following figure plots the expected best-case speedup for the same algorithm (calculated up to almost *n=10,000*). It does not matter how many processors we use; we cannot get a speedup greater than *100X*, meaning that the fastest our code will run is one second, which is the time its serial fraction takes on a single processor, exactly as predicted by Amdahl's law:

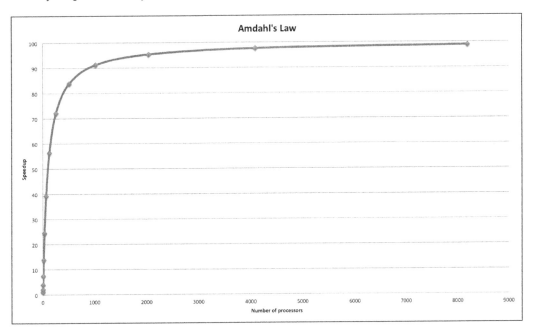

Amdahl's law tells us two things: how much of a speedup we can reasonably expect in the best-case scenario and when to stop throwing hardware at the problem because of diminishing returns.

Another interesting observation is that Amdahl's law applies equally to distributed systems and hybrid parallel-distributed systems as well. In those cases, *n* refers to the total number of processors across computers.

One aspect that should be mentioned at this point is that as the systems that we can use become more powerful, our distributed algorithms will take less and less time to run, if they can make use of the extra cycles.

When the runtime of our applications becomes reasonably short, what usually happens is that we tend to tackle bigger problems. This aspect of algorithm evolution, namely the expanding of the problem size (and therefore of the computing requirements) once acceptable performance levels are reached, is what is called **Gustafson's law**.

The mixed paradigm

Since most of the computers we buy today (2016) are multicore and often even both multiprocessor and multicore, any distributed application that we will write is likely to run on such systems. This brings us to being able to exploit both distributed computing and parallel computing techniques in our code. This mixed distributed-parallel paradigm is the de-facto standard nowadays when writing applications distributed over the network. As usual, reality is rarely binary.

Summary

We covered a lot of ground in this first chapter. We looked at parallelism and distributed computing. We saw some conceptual examples of both architectures and their pros and cons. We touched on their implications for memory access and noted that reality is oftentimes somewhere in between these two extremes. We finished the chapter by looking at Amdahl's law and its implications on scalability and the economics of throwing hardware at the problem. In the next chapters, we will put these concepts in practice and write some Python code!

2
Asynchronous Programming

In this chapter, we are finally going to write some code! The code in this chapter and all the chapters that follow is written for **Python 3.5** (the current release at the time of writing). When modules, syntaxes, or language constructs are not available in earlier versions of Python (for example, Python 2.7), these will be pointed out in this chapter. In general, however, the code presented here should work on Python 2.x with some minor modifications.

Let's go back to some of the ideas presented in the previous chapter. We know that we can structure our algorithms and programs so that they can run on a local machine or on one or more computers across a network. Even when our code runs on a single machine, as we saw, we can use multiple threads and/or multiple processes so that its various parts can run at the same time on multiple CPUs.

We will now pause thinking about multiple CPUs and instead look at a single thread/process of execution. There is a programming style called **asynchronous** or **nonblocking programming** that, in specific cases, leads to quite impressive performance gains when compared to the more traditional synchronous (or blocking) programming style.

Any computer program is conceptually composed of multiple tasks, each performing an operation. We can think of these tasks as functions and methods or even those individual steps that make up functions themselves. Examples of tasks could be dividing one number by another, printing something on a screen, or something more complex like fetching data from the Web, and so on.

Let's look at how these tasks use a CPU in a typical program. Let's consider a generic example of a piece of software composed of four tasks: A, B, C, and D. What these tasks do is not important at this stage. However, let's just assume that each of these four tasks does both some computation and some I/O. The most intuitive way of organizing these four tasks is to invoke them sequentially. The following figure shows, schematically, the CPU utilization of this simple four-task application:

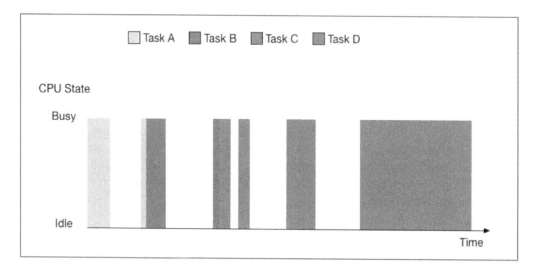

What we see in the preceding figure is that while each task performs its I/O operations, the CPU is sitting idle, waiting for the task to restart its computation. This leaves the CPU idle for a comparatively large amount of time.

The key observation here is that there is a dramatic difference (several orders of magnitude) in the speed at which we can move data from various components, such as disks, RAM, and the network, to the CPU.

The consequence of this massive difference in component bandwidth is that any code that handles significant I/O (disk access, network communication, and so on) has the risk of keeping the CPU idle for a large fraction of its execution time (as illustrated in the preceding figure).

The ideal situation would be to arrange our tasks so that when one task is waiting on I/O (that is, it is *blocking*), it is somehow suspended, and another one takes over the CPU. This is exactly what asynchronous (also called **event-driven**) programming is all about.

The following figure describes pictorially the reorganization of our conceptual four-task example using *asynchronous programming*:

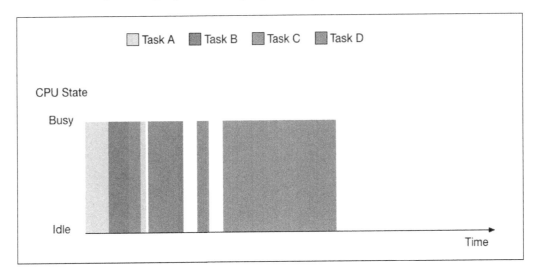

Here, the four tasks are still called sequentially, but instead of blocking each reserving the CPU for itself until they are done, they all *voluntarily* give up the CPU when they do not need it (because they are waiting on data). While there are still times when the CPU is idle, the overall runtime of our program is now noticeably faster.

It might be obvious, but it is worth pointing out that multithreaded programming would allow us to achieve the same efficiency by running tasks in parallel in different threads. However, there is a fundamental difference here: when using in a multi-threaded program, the operating system is the one deciding exactly threads are active and when they are superseded. In asynchronous programming, instead, each task can decide when to give up the CPU and therefore suspend its execution.

In addition, with asynchronous programming alone, we do not achieve true concurrency; there is still only one task running at any given time, which removes most race conditions from our code. Of course, nothing is stopping us from mixing paradigms and using multiple threads and/or multiple processes with asynchronous techniques within a single thread/process.

Another thing to keep in mind is that asynchronous programming really shines when dealing with I/O rather than CPU-intensive tasks (since there is not really a performance gain in suspending busy tasks).

Coroutines

In Python, the key to being able to suspend the execution of a function midway through is the use of **coroutines**, as we will see in this section. In order to understand coroutines, one needs to understand generators, and in order to understand those, one needs to have a grasp of iterators!

Most Python programmers are familiar with the concept of iterating some sort of collection (for example, strings, lists, tuples, file objects, and so on):

```
>>> for i in range(3):
...     print(i)
...
0
1
2
>>> for line in open('exchange_rates_v1.py'):
...     print(line, end='')
...
#!/usr/bin/env python3
import itertools
import time
import urllib.request
...
```

The reason why we can iterate all sorts of objects and not just lists or strings is the **iteration protocol**. The iteration protocol defines a standard interface for iteration: an object that implements __iter__ and __next__ (or __iter__ and next in Python 2.x) is an iterator and, as the name suggests, can be iterated over, as shown in the following code snippet:

```
class MyIterator(object):
    def __init__(self, xs):
        self.xs = xs

    def __iter__(self):
        return self

    def __next__(self):
        if self.xs:
```

```
            return self.xs.pop(0)
        else:
            raise StopIteration


for i in MyIterator([0, 1, 2]):
    print(i)
```

Running the preceding code prints the following output:

```
0
1
2
```

Again, the reason why we can loop over any instance of `MyIterator` is because it implements the iterator protocol by virtue of its __iter__ and __next__ methods; the former returns the object we iterate, and the latter method returns the individual elements of the sequence one by one.

To better see how the protocol works, we can unroll the loop manually as the following piece of code shows:

```
itrtr = MyIterator([3, 4, 5, 6])


print(next(itrtr))
print(next(itrtr))
print(next(itrtr))
print(next(itrtr))


print(next(itrtr))
```

Running the preceding code prints the following output:

```
3
4
5
6
Traceback (most recent call last):
  File "iteration.py", line 32, in <module>
    print(next(itrtr))
  File "iteration.py", line 19, in __next__
    raise StopIteration
StopIteration
```

We instantiate `MyIterator`, and then, in order to get its values, we call `next()` on it multiple times. Once the sequence is exhausted, `next()` throws a `StopIteration` exception. The `for` loop in Python, for instance, uses the same mechanism; it calls `next()` on its iterator and catches the `StopIteration` exception to know when to stop.

A generator is simply a callable that generates a sequence of results rather than *returning* a result. This is achieved by yielding (by way of using the `yield` keyword) the individual values rather then returning them, as we can see in the following example (`generators.py`):

```python
def mygenerator(n):
    while n:
        n -= 1
        yield n

if __name__ == '__main__':
    for i in mygenerator(3):
        print(i)
```

The preceding commands, when executed, give the following output:

```
2
1
0
```

It is the simple presence of `yield` that makes `mygenerator` a generator and not a simple function. The interesting behavior in the preceding code is that calling the `generator` function does not start the generation of the sequence at all; it just creates a `generator` object, as the following interpreter session shows:

```
>>> from generators import mygenerator
>>> mygenerator(5)
<generator object mygenerator at 0x101267b48>
```

In order to activate the `generator` object, we need to call `next()` on it, as we can see in the following snippets (in the same interpreter session):

```
>>> g = mygenerator(2)
>>> next(g)
1
>>> next(g)
0
>>> next(g)
Traceback (most recent call last):
  File "<stdin>", line 1, in <module>
StopIteration
```

Each `next()` call produces a value from the generated sequence until the sequence is empty, and that is when we get the `StopIteration` exception instead. This is the same behavior that we saw when we looked at iterators. Essentially, generators are a simple way to write iterators without the need for defining classes with their __iter__ and __next__ methods.

As a side note, you should keep in mind that generators are one-shot operations; it is not possible to iterate the generated sequence more than once. To do that, you have to call the `generator` function again.

The same `yield` expression used in `generator` functions to produce a sequence of values can be used on the right-hand side of an assignment to consume values. This allows the creation of coroutines. A coroutine is simply a type of function that can suspend and resume its execution at well-defined locations in its code (via `yield` expressions).

It is important to keep in mind that coroutines, despite being implemented as enhanced generators, are not conceptually generators themselves. The reason is that coroutines are not associated with iteration. Another way of looking at the difference is that generators produce values, whereas coroutines consume values.

Let's create some coroutines and see how we can use them. There are three main constructs in coroutines, which are stated as follows:

- `yield()`: This is used to suspend the execution of the coroutine
- `send()`: This is used to pass data to a coroutine (and hence resume its execution)
- `close()`: This is used to terminate a coroutine

The following code illustrates how we can use these in a silly coroutine (`coroutines.py`):

```
def complain_about(substring):
    print('Please talk to me!')
    try:
        while True:
            text = (yield)
            if substring in text:
                print('Oh no: I found a %s again!'
                    % (substring))
    except GeneratorExit:
        print('Ok, ok: I am quitting.')
```

We start off by defining our coroutine; it is just a function (we called it **complain_about**) that takes a single argument: a string. After printing a message, it enters an infinite loop enclosed in a `try except` clause. This means that the only way to exit the loop is via an exception. We are particularly interested in a very specific exception: `GeneratorExit`. When we catch one of these, we simply clean up and quit.

The body of the loop itself is pretty simple; we use a `yield` expression to fetch data (somehow) and store it in the variable `text`. Then, we simply check whether `substring` is in `text`, and if so, we whine a bit.

The following snippet shows how we can use this coroutine in the interpreter:

```
>>> from coroutines import complain_about
>>> c = complain_about('Ruby')
>>> next(c)
Please talk to me!
>>> c.send('Test data')
>>> c.send('Some more random text')
>>> c.send('Test data with Ruby somewhere in it')
Oh no: I found a Ruby again!
>>> c.send('Stop complaining about Ruby or else!')
Oh no: I found a Ruby again!
>>> c.close()
Ok, ok: I am quitting.
```

The execution of `complain_about('Ruby')` creates the coroutine, but nothing else seems to happen. In order to use the newly created coroutine, we need to call `next()` on it, just like we had to do with generators. In fact, we see that it is only after calling `next()` that we get **Please talk to me!** printed on the screen.

At this point, the coroutine has reached the `text = (yield)` line, which means that it suspends its execution. The control goes back to the interpreter so that we can send data to the coroutine itself. We do that using the its `send()` method, as the following snippet shows:

```
>>> c.send('Test data')
>>> c.send('Some more random text')
>>> c.send('Test data with Ruby somewhere in it')
Oh no: I found a Ruby again!
```

Each call of the send() method advances the code to the next yield; in our case, to the next iteration of the while loop and back to the text = (yield) line. At this point, the control goes back to the interpreter.

We can stop the coroutine by calling its close() method, which results in a GeneratorExit exception being risen inside the coroutine. The only thing that a coroutine is allowed to do at this point is catch the exception, do some cleaning up, and exit. The following snippet shows how to close the coroutine:

```
>>> c.close()
Ok, ok: I am quitting.
```

If we were to comment out the try...except block, we would not get the GeneratorExit exception back, but the coroutine will simply stop working, as the following snippet shows:

```
>>> def complain_about2(substring):
...     print('Please talk to me!')
...     while True:
...         text = (yield)
...         if substring in text:
...             print('Oh no: I found a %s again!'
...                 % (substring))
...
>>> c = complain_about2('Ruby')
>>> next(c)
Please talk to me!
>>> c.close()
>>> c.send('This will crash')
Traceback (most recent call last):
  File "<stdin>", line 1, in <module>
StopIteration
>>> next(c)
Traceback (most recent call last):
  File "<stdin>", line 1, in <module>
StopIteration
```

We see from the preceding example that once we close a coroutine, the object stays around, but it is not all that useful; we cannot send data to it, and we cannot use it by calling next().

When using coroutines, most people find having to call `next()` on the coroutine rather annoying and end up using a decorator to avoid the extra call, as the following example shows:

```
>>> def coroutine(fn):
...     def wrapper(*args, **kwargs):
...         c = fn(*args, **kwargs)
...         next(c)
...         return c
...     return wrapper
...
>>> @coroutine
... def complain_about2(substring):
...     print('Please talk to me!')
...     while True:
...         text = (yield)
...         if substring in text:
...             print('Oh no: I found a %s again!'
...                   % (substring))
...
>>> c = complain_about2('JavaScript')
Please talk to me!
>>> c.send('Test data with JavaScript somewhere in it')
Oh no: I found a JavaScript again!
>>> c.close()
```

Coroutines can be arranged in rather complex hierarchies, with one coroutine sending data to multiple other ones and getting data from multiple sources as well. They are particularly useful in network programming (for performance) and in system programming, where they can be used to reimplement most Unix tools very efficiently in pure Python.

An asynchronous example

To keep things simple but still interesting, let's write a tool that, given a text file, will count the occurrences of a given word. This example builds on the silly coroutine that we implemented in the previous section, adding some useful behavior to it.

It should be noted that, at least on a Linux or Mac OS X machine, one can achieve the same result very simply using the `grep` command, as we will see. Let's start by downloading a significantly large text that we will use as input data for our experiments. Let's just choose a public domain book from *Project Gutenberg: War and Peace* by Leo Tolstoy, which is freely available at `http://www.gutenberg.org/cache/epub/2600/pg2600.txt`.

The following snippet shows how we can download this text very easily:

```
$ curl -sO http://www.gutenberg.org/cache/epub/2600/pg2600.txt
$ wc pg2600.txt
   65007   566320 3291648 pg2600.txt
```

Next, we will start by counting the number of occurrences of the word *love*, regardless of case, in the file we just downloaded using `grep`, as the following snippet shows:

```
$ time (grep -io love pg2600.txt | wc -l)
677
(grep -io love pg2600.txt) 0.11s user 0.00s system 98% cpu 0.116 total
```

Let's now do the same thing in Python using coroutines, as shown in the following script (`grep.py`):

```python
def coroutine(fn):
    def wrapper(*args, **kwargs):
        c = fn(*args, **kwargs)
        next(c)
        return c
    return wrapper


def cat(f, case_insensitive, child):
    if case_insensitive:
        line_processor = lambda l: l.lower()
    else:
        line_processor = lambda l: l

    for line in f:
        child.send(line_processor(line))


@coroutine
```

```python
def grep(substring, case_insensitive, child):
    if case_insensitive:
        substring = substring.lower()
    while True:
        text = (yield)
        child.send(text.count(substring))


@coroutine
def count(substring):
    n = 0
    try:
        while True:
            n += (yield)
    except GeneratorExit:
        print(substring, n)


if __name__ == '__main__':
    import argparse

    parser = argparse.ArgumentParser()
    parser.add_argument('-i', action='store_true',
                        dest='case_insensitive')
    parser.add_argument('pattern', type=str)
    parser.add_argument('infile', type=argparse.FileType('r'))

    args = parser.parse_args()

    cat(args.infile, args.case_insensitive,
        grep(args.pattern, args.case_insensitive,
            count(args.pattern)))
```

Before we walk through the code, let's run it and see how it compares to grep:

```
$ time python3.5 grep.py -i love pg2600.txt
love 677
python3.5 grep.py -i love pg2600.txt  0.09s user 0.01s system 97% cpu
0.097 total
```

As we saw, our pure Python version that uses coroutines is competitive with the Unix grep command piped into wc for counting lines. Of course, the Unix grep command is significantly more powerful than our simple Python version. We cannot simply claim that Python is faster than C! At the same time, this is a pretty impressive result.

Let's walk through the code and see what is going on. We start off by reimplementing the coroutine decorator we saw earlier. After that, we break the problem into three distinct steps:

- Reading the file line by line (done by the cat function)
- Counting the occurrences of substring in each line (the grep coroutine)
- Adding up all the numbers and printing out the total (the count coroutine)

In the main body of the script, we parse command-line options and then pipe the output of cat to grep and the output of grep to count, just like we would do with regular Unix tools.

This chaining is done very simply; we pass the coroutine that receives data as an argument (child in the preceding example) to the function or coroutine that produces the data. We then, inside the data source, simply call the send coroutine method.

The first function, cat, acts as the data source for the whole program; it reads the file line by line and sends each line to grep (child.send(line)). If we want a case-insensitive match, then we simply make line lowercase; otherwise, we pass it unchanged.

The grep command is our first coroutine. In it, we enter an infinite loop where we keep receiving data (text = (yield)), count the occurrences of substring in text, and send that number of occurrences to the next coroutine (count in our case): child.send(text.count(substring))).

The count coroutine keeps a running total, n, of the numbers it receives, (n += (yield)), from grep. It catches the GeneratorExit exception sent to each coroutine when they are closed (which in our case happens automatically when we reach the end of the file) to know when to print out substring and n.

Things become interesting when we start organizing coroutines into complex graphs. For instance, we might want to count the concurrence of multiple words in the input file.

The following code shows one way of doing this via a single extra coroutine responsible for broadcasting its input to an arbitrary number of child coroutines (mgrep.py):

```python
def coroutine(fn):
    def wrapper(*args, **kwargs):
        c = fn(*args, **kwargs)
        next(c)
        return c
    return wrapper


def cat(f, case_insensitive, child):
    if case_insensitive:
        line_processor = lambda l: l.lower()
    else:
        line_processor = lambda l: l

    for line in f:
        child.send(line_processor(line))


@coroutine
def grep(substring, case_insensitive, child):
    if case_insensitive:
        substring = substring.lower()
    while True:
        text = (yield)
        child.send(text.count(substring))


@coroutine
def count(substring):
    n = 0
    try:
        while True:
            n += (yield)
    except GeneratorExit:
        print(substring, n)


@coroutine
def fanout(children):
    while True:
```

```
        data = (yield)
        for child in children:
            child.send(data)


if __name__ == '__main__':
    import argparse

    parser = argparse.ArgumentParser()
    parser.add_argument('-i', action='store_true',
                        dest='case_insensitive')
    parser.add_argument('patterns', type=str, nargs='+',)
    parser.add_argument('infile', type=argparse.FileType('r'))

    args = parser.parse_args()

    cat(args.infile, args.case_insensitive,
        fanout([grep(p, args.case_insensitive,
                     count(p)) for p in args.patterns]))
```

The code is virtually identical to the previous example (grep.py). Let's look at the differences. We define the broadcaster: fanout. The fanout() coroutine takes a list of coroutines as input and then sits (as usual) in an infinite loop waiting for data. Once it receives data (data = (yield)), it simply sends it to all registered coroutines (for child in children: child.send(data)).

Without changing the code for cat, grep, and count, we are able to generalize our program and search for an arbitrary number of strings in our text!

Performance is still very good, as the following snippet shows:

```
$ time python3.5 mgrep.py -i love hate hope pg2600.txt
hate 103
love 677
hope 158
python3.5 mgrep.py -i love hate hope pg2600.txt   0.16s user 0.01s system
98% cpu 0.166 total
```

Summary

Python has had support for asynchronous programming since version 1.5.2, with the introduction of the `asyncore` and `asynchat` modules for asynchronous network programming. Version 2.5 introduced the ability to send data to coroutines via `yield` expressions, allowing us to write asynchronous code in a simpler but more powerful way. Python 3.4 introduced a new library for asynchronous I/O called **asyncio**.

Python 3.5 introduced true coroutine types via `async def` and `await`. Interested readers are encouraged to explore these new developments. One word of warning though: asynchronous programming is a powerful tool that can dramatically improve the performance of I/O-intensive code. It does not come without issues, though, the main of which is complexity.

Any important asynchronous code has to carefully select nonblocking libraries in order to avoid using blocking code. It has to implement a coroutine scheduler (since the OS does not schedule coroutines for us like it does with threads), which involves writing an event loop and adding further complexity. Reading asynchronous code can be challenging to the point that even our simple examples do not look all that simple at first sight. Handle with care!

3

Parallelism in Python

We mentioned threads, processes, and in general, parallel programming in the previous two chapters. We talked, at a very high level and very much in abstract terms, about how you can organize code so that some portions run in parallel, potentially on multiple CPUs or even multiple machines.

In this chapter, we will look at parallel programming in more detail and see which facilities Python offers us to make our code use more than one CPU or CPU core at the time (but always within the boundaries of a single machine). The main goal here will be speed for CPU-intensive problems, and responsiveness for I/O-intensive code.

The good news is that we can write parallel programs in Python using just modules in the standard library and nothing else. This is not to say that no external libraries and tools might be relevant—quite the opposite. It is just that the Standard Library is enough for what we will try and do in this chapter.

In this chapter, we will cover the following topics:

- Multiple threads
- Multiple processes
- Multiprocess queues

Multiple threads

Python has had support for threads for a very long time now (at least since version 1.4). It also offers a robust high-level interface to OS-native (that is, **POSIX** on Linux and Mac OS X) threads in the *threading* module, which is what we will use for the examples in this section.

It should be noted that on single CPU systems, the use of multiple threads would not give true concurrency, since only one thread will be executed at any given point in time (remember that a CPU runs only one task at any given point in time). It is only on a multiprocessor system that threads can run in parallel. We will assume that we will make use of a multiprocessor/multicore system for the remainder of the chapter.

Let's start by writing a simple program that makes use of multiple threads to download data from the Web. In your favorite editor, create a new Python script (currency.py) with the following code:

```python
from threading import Thread
from queue import Queue
import urllib.request



URL = 'http://finance.yahoo.com/d/quotes.csv?s={}=X&f=p'



def get_rate(pair, outq, url_tmplt=URL):
    with urllib.request.urlopen(url_tmplt.format(pair)) as res:
        body = res.read()
    outq.put((pair, float(body.strip())))



if __name__ == '__main__':
    import argparse

    parser = argparse.ArgumentParser()
    parser.add_argument('pairs', type=str, nargs='+')
    args = parser.parse_args()

    outputq = Queue()
```

```
for pair in args.pairs:
    t = Thread(target=get_rate,
                kwargs={'pair': pair,
                        'outq': outputq})
    t.daemon = True
    t.start()

for _ in args.pairs:
    pair, rate = outputq.get()
    print(pair, rate)
    outputq.task_done()
outputq.join()
```

What is going on in the preceding code is pretty simple. We start by importing the modules we need from the Standard Library (that is, `threading`, `queue`, and `urllib.request`). We then define a simple function (`get_rate`) that gives a currency pair (that is, EURUSD for Euros versus US dollars or CHFAUS for Swiss Francs versus Australian dollars) and a thread-safe queue (that is, an instance of `Queue` from the Python `queue` module), connects to Yahoo! Finance and downloads the last published exchange rate for that currency pair.

The call to the Yahoo! Finance API returns plain text with the desired number and a carriage return (or, more precisely, it returns the content of a CSV file with just the exchange rate). This means that we do not need to worry about parsing HTML, and we can instead simply cast the text we get to a floating point number and get our exchange rate out.

The main portion of our script uses, as usual, the `argparse` module to parse command-line arguments. It then creates a queue (which we call `outputq`) to hold the data produced by the various threads that download the exchange rates. Once we have the output queue, we then spawn a new worker thread for each currency pair. Each worker thread simply runs the `get_rate` function, with a currency pair and the output queue as arguments.

Since these threads are just *fire and forget* threads, we can make them daemons, meaning that the main Python program will not wait for them to quit (`join` in thread parlance) before exiting.

It is quite important to get this last observation about daemon threads and queues right. The main difficulty in using threads to perform actions in parallel is that we cannot tell when a given thread will read or write any data shared with other threads.

This can give rise to what is usually called a **race condition**. This is the situation where on one hand, the correct execution of the system depends on some actions being performed in a given order, and on the other hand, these actions are not guaranteed to happen in the right order, that is, the order envisioned by the programmer.

A simple example of a race condition is what can happen in reference-counting algorithms. In a reference-counting, garbage-collected interpreter such as **CPython** (the standard Python interpreter), every object has a counter, keeping track of how many references to that object currently exist.

Every time a reference to any object is created, the corresponding reference counter is incremented by 1. Every time a reference is deleted, the counter is decremented by 1. Once the counter goes to 0, the associated object is deallocated. Attempts to use a deallocated object usually result in a segmentation fault.

This means that we somehow need to enforce a strict order of reference counter increments and decrements. Imagine two threads getting a reference to an object for a few moments and then deleting it. If both threads access the same reference counter at the same time, they could overwrite its value, as the following example illustrates:

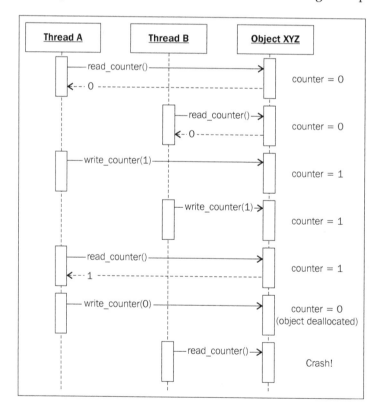

One way out of synchronization problems like these is the use of locks. Thread-safe queues are a very convenient example of lock-based data structures that we can use to organize data access.

Since each thread writes to the same output queue, we might just as well monitor that queue to know when results are ready and it is time to quit. In the preceding code, we do that by simply fetching one result from the queue per currency pair (the loop over `args.pairs`) and by waiting for the queue to join (`outputq.join()`), which will happen when all the results have been fetched (more precisely, when each `get()` method is followed by a call to `task_done()`). This way, we are sure that our program does not quit prematurely.

While this code is just an example-grade code and lacks error checking, retries, missing or invalid data handling, and so on, it still shows a useful, queue-based, architecture. It should be noted, however, that using lock-based queues to orchestrate data access and avoid race conditions could be expensive, depending on the application.

The following figure illustrates the architecture of this simple example, with three worker threads retrieving the exchange rate for three currency pairs and storing the name of the pair and the corresponding exchange rate in the output queue:

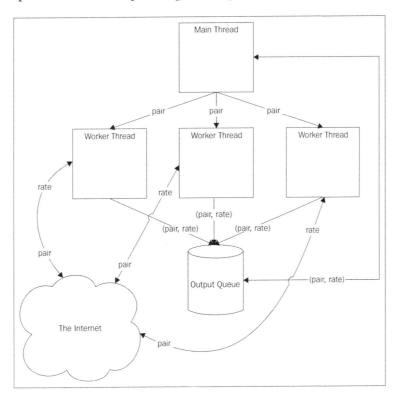

We could, of course, avoid spawning threads and simply call our `get_rate` function once for each currency pair and get the exchange rates sequentially. If we start the Python interpreter, we can do just that, as the following snippet shows:

```
>>> from currency import get_rate
>>> import queue
>>> from time import time
>>> q = queue.Queue()
>>> pairs = ('EURUSD', 'GBPUSD', 'CHFEUR')
>>> t0 = time(); [get_rate(p, q) for p in pairs]; dt = time() - t0
[None, None, None]
>>> dt
1.1785249710083008
>>> [q.get() for p in pairs]
[('EURUSD', 1.1042), ('GBPUSD', 1.5309), ('CHFEUR', 0.9176)]
```

It takes approximately 1.2 seconds to get the exchange rates for three currencies, one request at a time.

Let's try to run our thread-based example on the same three currency pairs (on a qaud-core machine) and see what happens:

```
$ time python3.5 currency.py EURUSD GBPUSD CHFEUR
EURUSD 1.1042
GBPUSD 1.5309
CHFEUR 0.9176
python3.5 currency.py EURUSD GBPUSD CHFEUR  0.08s user 0.02s system 26%
cpu 0.380 total
```

Why is our code essentially three times faster than the sequential version in the interpreter (0.4 seconds versus 1.2 seconds)? The reason is that, by using threads, we are able to execute the three web requests in parallel. Of course, there is an overhead in spawning threads and using queues (remember Amdahl's law? These overheads are part of the serial component of our algorithm), but still, even for this simple application, we can see that parallelism, and threads in particular, can give a significant boost in performance. As a side note, we could have achieved the same result using coroutines and nonblocking sockets on one CPU, as we saw in the previous chapter.

Before we get too excited, let's look at another example where the use of threads results in no performance gain whatsoever. Create a new Python script (`fib.py`) using the following code:

```python
from threading import Thread


def fib(n):
    if n <= 2:
        return 1
    elif n == 0:
        return 0
    elif n < 0:
        raise Exception('fib(n) is undefined for n < 0')
    return fib(n - 1) + fib(n - 2)


if __name__ == '__main__':
    import argparse

    parser = argparse.ArgumentParser()
    parser.add_argument('-n', type=int, default=1)
    parser.add_argument('number', type=int, nargs='?', default=34)
    args = parser.parse_args()

    assert args.n >= 1, 'The number of threads has to be > 1'
    for i in range(args.n):
        t = Thread(target=fib, args=(args.number,))
        t.start()
```

Given what we have seen so far, this piece of code is very simple to understand; we ask our users for the number of threads to start, and then, we ask each thread to compute the `args.number` Fibonacci number. We do not really care about Fibonacci numbers (as shown by the fact that we do not even store them anywhere); we just want to perform some CPU-intensive computation, and calculating Fibonacci numbers is as good as any other task.

Let's run the preceding example for various levels of concurrency and see what happens, as the following snippet shows:

```
$ time python3.5 ./fib.py -n 1 34
python3.5 ./fib.py -n 1 34  2.00s user 0.01s system 99% cpu 2.013 total
$ time python3.5 ./fib.py -n 2 34
python3.5 ./fib.py -n 2 34  4.38s user 0.04s system 100% cpu 4.414 total
$ time python3.5 ./fib.py -n 3 34
python3.5 ./fib.py -n 3 34  6.28s user 0.08s system 100% cpu 6.354 total
$ time python3.5 ./fib.py -n 4 34
python3.5 ./fib.py -n 4 34  8.47s user 0.11s system 100% cpu 8.541 total
```

Interesting! The use of two threads to compute the 34 Fibonacci number in parallel takes twice as much time as using a single thread to do the same computation once. Increasing the number of parallel computations just increases the execution time linearly. Clearly, something is not quite right, as we would have expected the threads to run in parallel (again, on a quad-core machine).

It turns out that there is something not obvious going on deep inside the Python interpreter that is affecting our CPU-bound threads. That thing is called **Global Interpreter Lock** (GIL). As the name implies, the GIL is a global lock that is used, mostly, to keep reference counting sane (remember when we talked about that a little while ago?). The consequence of the GIL is that even though Python threads are real OS-native threads, only one of them can be active at any given point in time.

This has led some to say that the Python interpreter is a single-threaded interpreter, which is not quite true. However, this statement is also, conceptually at least, not completely wrong either. The situation we just witnessed is very similar to the behavior we observed when writing coroutines. In that case, in fact, only one piece of code could run at any given point in time. Things *just work*, meaning we get the parallelism that we expect, when one coroutine or thread waits for I/O and another one takes over the CPU. Things do not work as well in terms of performance speedups, when one task needs the CPU for a long time, as is the case with CPU-bound tasks as in the Fibonacci example.

Just like with coroutines, using threads in Python is far from being a lost cause. Parallel I/O can give a significant performance boost to our application, both in the case of code using multiple threads or coroutines. GUI-based applications benefit from using threads as well; one thread can handle updates to the GUI, while another one can perform actions in the background without freezing the user interface. It is just that one needs to be aware of the effects of the GIL in the standard Python interpreter and plan accordingly. As a side note, not all Python interpreters have the GIL; **Jython**, for instance, does not.

Multiple processes

Traditionally, the way Python programmers have worked around the GIL and its effect on CPU-bound threads has been to use multiple processes instead of multiple threads. This approach (multiprocessing) has some disadvantages, which mostly boil down to having to launch multiple instances of the Python interpreter with all the startup time and memory usage penalties that this implies.

At the same time, however, using multiple processes to execute tasks in parallel has some nice properties. Multiple processes have their own memory space and implement a *share-nothing architecture*, making it easy to reason about data-access patterns. They also allow us to (more) easily transition from a single-machine architecture to a distributed application, where one would have to use multiple processes (on different machines) anyway.

There are two main modules in the Python Standard Library that we can use to implement process-based parallelism, and both of them are truly excellent. One is called **multiprocessing** and the other is concurrent.futures. The concurrent. futures module is built on top of multiprocessing and the threading module and provides a powerful high-level interface to them.

We will use the high-level concurrent.futures package for the next example. Python 2.x users are able to install it as an external package (that is, futures, available in the Python Package Index Repository).

To get started, let's implement the exact same Fibonacci example that we saw in the previous section, this time using multiple processes. At the same time, we will get a quick introduction to the concurrent.futures module.

Create a new script (mpfib.py) using the following code:

```python
import concurrent.futures as cf
```

```python
def fib(n):
    if n <= 2:
        return 1
    elif n == 0:
        return 0
    elif n < 0:
        raise Exception('fib(n) is undefined for n < 0')
```

```
    return fib(n - 1) + fib(n - 2)


if __name__ == '__main__':
    import argparse

    parser = argparse.ArgumentParser()
    parser.add_argument('-n', type=int, default=1)
    parser.add_argument('number', type=int, nargs='?', default=34)
    args = parser.parse_args()

    assert args.n >= 1, 'The number of threads has to be > 1'
    with cf.ProcessPoolExecutor(max_workers=args.n) as pool:
        results = pool.map(fib, [args.number] * args.n)
```

The code is remarkably compact and very readable. Looking at just the differences with multithreaded code, we see that after getting the command-line parameters, we simply create a `ProcessPoolExecutor` instance and call its `map()` method to perform computations in parallel.

Intuitively, we created a pool of `args.n` worker processes and used that pool to execute our `fib` function on each item of the input list (which is just `args.number` repeated `args.n` times), potentially in parallel (depending, of course, on the number of CPUs that we have).

Running the preceding code in the terminal (on a quad-core laptop) is quite interesting, as the following code snippet shows:

```
$ time python3.5 ./mpfib.py -n 1 34
python3.5 ./mpfib.py -n 1 34  1.89s user 0.02s system 99% cpu 1.910 total
$ time python3.5 ./mpfib.py -n 2 34
python3.5 ./mpfib.py -n 2 34  3.76s user 0.02s system 196% cpu 1.928
total
$ time python3.5 ./mpfib.py -n 3 34
python3.5 ./mpfib.py -n 3 34  5.70s user 0.03s system 291% cpu 1.964
total
$ time python3.5 ./mpfib.py -n 4 34
python3.5 ./mpfib.py -n 4 34  7.71s user 0.03s system 386% cpu 2.006
total
```

As we can see, running our example code on a machine with four hardware cores, we can truly execute more than one computation in parallel to the point where the execution times for args.n between one and four stay the same.

Starting more processes than there are hardware cores introduces significant performance degradation, as the following example shows:

```
$ time python3.5 ./mpfib.py -n 8 34

python3.5 ./mpfib.py -n 8 34  30.23s user 0.06s system 755% cpu 4.011
total

$ time python3.5 ./mpfib.py -n 16 34

python3.5 ./mpfib.py -n 16 34  63.78s user 0.13s system 758% cpu 8.424
total
```

Going back to the code and looking at the last two lines in more detail, we see that there are quite a few things happening. First, we use the ProcessPoolExecutor class exported by concurrent.futures. This is one of the two main classes exported by the module, the other being ThreadPoolExecutor, which is used to create a pool of threads, instead of a pool of processes.

Both, ProcessPoolExecutor and ThreadPoolExecutor have the same fundamental API (and in fact, they are both subclasses of the same class): they have three main methods, which are as follows:

- submit(f, *args, **kwargs): This is used to schedule an asynchronous call to f(*args, **kwargs) and return a Future instance as a result placeholder.
- map(f, *arglist, timeout=None, chunksize=1): This is the equivalent to the built-in map(f, *arglist) method. It returns a list of Future objects rather than a list of actual results, as map would do.

The third method, shutdown(wait=True) is used to free the resources used by the Executor object as soon as all currently scheduled functions are done. It waits (if wait=True) until that happens. Using an Executor object after a call to this method will raise a RuntimeError exception.

Executor objects can also be used as context managers (as we are, in the preceding example, using with cf.ProcessPoolExecutor(max_workers=args.n) as pool construct). In those cases, there is an implicit blocking call made to the Executor shutdown method on the context manager's exit. This means that if we were to access the results list, we would get integers rather than Future instances once the context manager exits.

A `Future` instance, the other main class exported by the `concurrent.futures` package, is a placeholder for the result of an asynchronous call. We can check whether the call is still running, whether or not it raised an exception, and so on. We call a Future instance `result()` method to access (with an optional timeout) its value once it is ready.

It is instructive to reimplement the same Fibonacci example without using a context manager. This way, we can see the `Future` class at work. We can do this in the interpreter, as the following snippet shows:

```
>>> from mpfib import fib
>>> from concurrent.futures import ProcessPoolExecutor
>>> pool = ProcessPoolExecutor(max_workers=1)
>>> fut = pool.submit(fib, 38)
>>> fut
<Future at 0x101b74128 state=running>
>>> fut.running()
True
>>> fut.done()
False
>>> fut.result(timeout=0)
Traceback (most recent call last):
  File "<stdin>", line 1, in <module>
  File "/Library/Frameworks/Python.framework/Versions/3.5/lib/python3.5/
concurrent/futures/_base.py", line 407, in result
    raise TimeoutError()
concurrent.futures._base.TimeoutError
>>> fut.result(timeout=None)
39088169
>>> fut
<Future at 0x101b74128 state=finished returned int>
>>> fut.done()
True
>>> fut.running()
False
>>> fut.cancelled()
False
>>> fut.exception()
```

In the preceding interpreter session, we see how to use the `concurrent.futures` package to create a worker pool (using the `ProcessPoolExecutor` class) and submit work to it (`pool.submit(fib, 38)`). As we expect, `submit` returns a `Future` object (`fut` in the preceding code), which is a placeholder for a result that is not yet available.

We inspect `fut` to check whether it is still running (`fut.running()`), done, (`fut.done()`), or cancelled (`fut.cancelled()`). If we try and ask for its result before it is ready (`fut.result(timeout=0)`), we get a `TimeoutError` exception. This means that we either have to wait for the `Future` object to be available or ask for its result without a timeout, which is what we do in `fut.result(timeout=None)`, which blocks until the `Future` object is ready. Since our code runs without errors, `fut.exception()` returns `None`.

We can make a one-line modification to our process-based parallel code and switch to using threads instead; simply replace `ProcessPoolExecutor` with `ThreadPoolExecutor`. For a quick example, change the previous script (`mpfib.py`), replacing the following line:

```
with cf.ProcessPoolExecutor(max_workers=args.n) as pool:
```

Replace the preceding line with this one:

```
with cf.ThreadPoolExecutor(max_workers=args.n) as pool:
```

The result (let's call it `mtfib.py`) has, as expected, the same performance behavior as our multithreaded Fibonacci example from the previous section (`fib.py`), as the following snippet demonstrates:

```
$ time python3.5 ./mtfib.py -n 1 34
python3.5 ./mtfib.py -n 1 34   2.04s user 0.01s system 99% cpu 2.059 total
$ time python3.5 ./mtfib.py -n 2 34
python3.5 ./mtfib.py -n 2 34   4.43s user 0.04s system 100% cpu 4.467 total
$ time python3.5 ./mtfib.py -n 3 34
python3.5 ./mtfib.py -n 3 34   6.69s user 0.06s system 100% cpu 6.720 total
$ time python3.5 ./mtfib.py -n 4 34
python3.5 ./mtfib.py -n 4 34   8.98s user 0.10s system 100% cpu 9.022 total
```

Multiprocess queues

When using multiple processes, the issue that comes up is how to exchange data between the workers. The multiprocessing module offers a mechanism to do that in the form of queues and pipes. Hence, we are going to look at multiprocess queues.

The multiprocessing.Queue class is modeled after the queue.Queue class with the additional twist that items stored in the multiprocessing queue need to be pickable. To illustrate how to use these queues, create a new Python script (queues.py) with the following code:

```python
import multiprocessing as mp


def fib(n):
    if n <= 2:
        return 1
    elif n == 0:
        return 0
    elif n < 0:
        raise Exception('fib(n) is undefined for n < 0')
    return fib(n - 1) + fib(n - 2)


def worker(inq, outq):
    while True:
        data = inq.get()
        if data is None:
            return
        fn, arg = data
        outq.put(fn(arg))


if __name__ == '__main__':
    import argparse

    parser = argparse.ArgumentParser()
    parser.add_argument('-n', type=int, default=1)
```

```
parser.add_argument('number', type=int, nargs='?', default=34)
args = parser.parse_args()

assert args.n >= 1, 'The number of threads has to be > 1'

tasks = mp.Queue()
results = mp.Queue()
for i in range(args.n):
    tasks.put((fib, args.number))

for i in range(args.n):
    mp.Process(target=worker, args=(tasks, results)).start()

for i in range(args.n):
    print(results.get())

for i in range(args.n):
    tasks.put(None)
```

At this point, you should be extremely familiar with the code; we are still computing Fibonacci numbers using the same old (and terribly inefficient) recursive function that we already saw a few times. We use a two-queue architecture, whereby one queue holds the tasks to be performed (in this case, the function to be called and its only argument), while the other queue holds the results (simple integers in this example).

As we did previously, we use a sentinel value (None) in the task queue to signal that the worker processes should quit. The worker process is a simple multiprocessing. Process instance whose target is the worker function and whose behavior is the one that we just described.

The performance characteristics of this queue-based example are the same as the queue-less script (mpfib.py) at the beginning of this section, as the following terminal session shows:

```
$ time python3.5 ./queues.py -n 1 34
5702887
python3.5 ./queues.py -n 1 34  1.87s user 0.02s system 99% cpu 1.890
total
$ time python3.5 ./queues.py -n 4 34
```

```
5702887 (repeated 4 times)

python3.5 ./queues.py -n 4 34   7.66s user 0.03s system 383% cpu 2.005
total

$ time python3.5 ./queues.py -n 8 34

5702887 (repeated 8 times)

python3.5 ./queues.py -n 8 34  30.46s user 0.06s system 762% cpu 4.003
total
```

For our little example, adding a couple of queues in the mix does not introduce measurable performance degradation.

Closing thoughts

One of the main difficulties in developing parallel applications is getting data access right and avoiding race conditions or situations that would corrupt shared data. Sometimes, these situations are easy to spot as they lead to spectacular crashes. Other times, more worryingly, they are not—the application keeps plodding along, producing incorrect results.

It is always important to have good tests for our applications and their internal functions. It is even more so for parallel applications, where building a clear mental picture of what happens where and when can be particularly challenging.

Another difficulty in parallelizing algorithms is to know when to stop. Amdahl's law tells us very clearly that parallelization is, from a given point forward, a game of diminishing returns. Experience tells us that parallelization efforts can easily become a time sink. It is important to have clarity in our minds as to which parts of the code need to be parallelized (if any) and what the theoretical maximum speedup is.

It is only then that we can decide when to stop pouring time and energy into improving the performance of a given algorithm. Furthermore, sometimes, using an existing parallel library (such as NumPy) provides the best cost-rewards ratio.

As a side note, and as mentioned briefly at the beginning of the book, a way to offset the diminishing returns predicted by Amdahl's law is to increase the size of the problem as the total performance of the system increases (which is a very natural tendency of us scientists and engineers).

Of course, as our applications perform more work, the contribution of any setup, coordination and cleanup work (which is typically serial) to the overall performance decreases. This, again, is the heart of Gustafson's law.

Summary

We looked at a couple of technologies that we can exploit to make our Python code run faster and, in some cases, use multiple CPUs in our computers. One of these is the use of multiple threads, and the other is the use of multiple processes. Both are supported natively by the Python standard library.

We looked at three modules: `threading`, for developing multithreaded applications, `multiprocessing`, for developing process-based parallelism, and `concurrent.futures`, which provides a high-level asynchronous interface to both.

As far as parallelism goes, these three modules are not the only ones that exist in Python land. Other packages implement their own parallel strategies internally, freeing programmers from doing so themselves. Probably, the best known of these is NumPy, the de-facto standard Python package for array and matrix manipulations. Depending on the BLAS library that it is compiled against, NumPy is able to use multiple threads to speed up complex operations (for example, the matrix-matrix dot product).

In the same vein, one interesting thing to note is that the `multiprocessing` module also has support for Python processes running on different machines and communicating over the network. In particular, it exports a couple of `Manager` classes (that is, `BaseManager` and `SyncManager`). These use a socket server to manage data and queues and share them over the network. The interested reader can explore this topic further by reading the online documentation in the multiprocessing module section available at `https://docs.python.org/3/library/multiprocessing.html#managers`.

Another piece of technology that might be worth investigating is Cython, a Python-like language to create `C` modules that is extremely popular and actively developed. Cython has excellent support for **OpenMP**, a directive-based API for C, C++, and Fortran, that allows programmers to easily multithread their code.

4

Distributed Applications – with Celery

This chapter is a follow up on some of the topics that we discussed so far. In particular, it explores asynchronous programming and distributed computing in detail with some example applications. It concentrates on **Celery**, a sophisticated Python framework that is used to build distributed applications. Toward the end, the chapter explores some alternative packages to Celery: **Pyro** and **Python-RQ**.

You should be familiar, at this point, with the basic ideas behind parallelism, distributed computing, and asynchronous programming. If not, it might be worthwhile to skim the previous chapters to get a refresher.

Establishing a multimachine environment

The first thing to do before we dive into Celery and the other Python packages that we will explore is set up a test environment. We are developing distributed applications, which means that we ideally need a multimachine environment.

Those of you who have access to at least two machines in a properly set up network environment (meaning that these test machines have DNS-resolvable names) can skip to the next section. All the rest, please keep reading.

For those without easy access to multiple machines for development and testing, there are still a number of solutions that are easy to implement and either free or very inexpensive.

One is to simply use virtual machines running on the local host (for instance, using VirtualBox: https://www.virtualbox.org). Just create a couple of VMs, install your favorite Linux distribution on it, and keep them running in the background. Since these do not need a graphical desktop for development purposes, they can be very lightweight in terms of RAM and number of cores assigned to them.

Another option could be to buy a couple of inexpensive tiny computer boards, such as the **Raspberry Pi** (https://www.raspberrypi.org), install Linux on them, and put them on the local network.

A third solution could be to sign up for an account with a cloud provider, such as **Amazon EC2**, and use some of their on-demand virtual machines. If you are going down this route, make sure that the network ports used by the various packages we are going to play with are open in your firewall.

Regardless of how you get a hold of your development machines, some of you will now face the inconvenience of not having a full DNS setup on your network. In this case, the simplest solution is editing the /etc/hosts files on all machines for a local name resolution. Just look up the IP addresses of the hosts we want to use, decide on simple names for each host, and add them to /etc/hosts (on all computers).

This is my hosts file for when I use two virtual machines on my Mac machine:

```
$ cat /etc/hosts
##
# Host Database
#
# localhost is used to configure the loopback interface
# when the system is booting.  Do not change this entry.
##
127.0.0.1 localhost
255.255.255.255 broadcasthost
::1             localhost
fe80::1%lo0 localhost

# Development VMs
192.168.123.150 ubuntu1 ubuntu1.local
192.168.123.151 ubuntu2 ubuntu2.local
```

Similarly, this is the host file on each of my two virtual machines (running on Ubuntu 15.04):

```
$ cat /etc/hosts
127.0.0.1 localhost
192.168.123.151 ubuntu2
192.168.123.150 ubuntu1


# The following lines are desirable for IPv6 capable hosts
::1     ip6-localhost ip6-loopback
fe00::0 ip6-localnet
ff00::0 ip6-mcastprefix
ff02::1 ip6-allnodes
ff02::2 ip6-allrouters
```

You should make sure that the IP addresses and names in your hosts files reflect the ones on the machines you decide to use. For the rest of the book, we will simply refer to these machines as HOST1, HOST2, HOST3, and so on.

Armed with at least a couple of machines (real or virtual) that we can access over the network, we can proceed to write some distributed applications!

Installing Celery

Celery (http://www.celeryproject.org) is the first third-party library that we encounter in this book, since so far, we have only looked at modules and packages in the Python standard library. Celery is a distributed task queue, meaning that it is a queue-based system like some of the ones that we built in the previous chapters. It is also distributed, which means that worker processes, as well as the queues holding results and work requests, typically run on different machines.

Let's start by installing Celery and its dependencies. We start by setting up a virtual environment on each machine (let's call it book so that we know it is related to the examples in this book), as shown in the following line of code (assuming a Unix environment):

```
$ pip install virtualenvwrapper
```

If the preceding command fails with a permission denied error, then you can use sudo to install virtualenvwrapper as a super-user, as shown in the following command:

```
$ sudo pip install virtualenvwrapper
```

The sudo command will ask for our Unix user password. Alternatively, one could install the virtualenvwrapper package locally using the following command:

```
$ pip install --user virtualenvwrapper
```

Whatever solution we choose, once we have virtualenvwrapper installed, we need to configure it by defining three environment variables, as shown in the following command (for bash-like shells and assuming virtualenvwrapper.sh was installed in /usr/local/bin):

```
$ export WORKON_HOME=$HOME/venvs
$ export PROJECT_HOME=$HOME/workspace
$ source /usr/local/bin/virtualenvwrapper.sh
```

You should change the preceding paths to reflect where you want your virtual environments to live ($WORKON_HOME) and their code root directory ($PROJECT_HOME) to be. The full path to virtualenvwrapper.sh might need to be changed as well. The preceding three lines are best added to relevant shell startup files (for example, ~/.bashrc or ~/.profile).

Once the preceding configuration is taken care of, we can create the virtual environment that we will use for the rest of the book, as shown in this code:

```
$ mkvirtualenv book --python=`which python3.5`
```

The preceding command will create a new virtual environment under $WORKON_HOME called book, using Python 3.5, and activate it. In future, we can always activate this virtual environment using the workon command, as shown in the following line of code:

```
$ workon book
```

The advantage of using virtual environments is that we can install all the packages we want without *polluting* our system's Python installation. If, at some point in the future, we decide that we do not need a given virtual environment any longer, we can simply delete it (refer to the rmvirtualenv command).

Now, we are ready to install Celery. As usual, we will be using pip, as demonstrated in the following code (to be executed on each machine):

```
$ pip install celery
```

The preceding pip command will download, unpack, and install Celery and all its dependencies in the currently active virtual environment (in our case, book).

We are almost there; we just need to install and configure a broker that Celery will use to host the task queue(s) and deliver messages to worker processes (this needs to be done on just one machine, say HOST1). As we can see from the documentation, Celery supports a number of brokers, including **SQLAlchemy** (http://www.sqlalchemy.org) for local development and testing. The recommended broker, however, is **RabbitMQ** (https://www.rabbitmq.com), and that is the one we are going to use in this book.

Head over to https://www.rabbitmq.com for installation instructions, documentation, and downloads. On a Mac machine, the simplest way to install it is to use **homebrew** (http://brew.sh), as shown in this command:

```
$ brew install rabbitmq
```

For Windows systems, one is probably better off using the official installer. For Linux, official native packages are available.

Once RabbitMQ in installed, it should work out of the box. There is a simple configuration step that is only necessary here because for these examples, we will not bother creating users with passwords to access the queues. Just edit (or create) the RabbitMQ configuration file (typically located at /usr/local/etc/rabbitmq/rabbitmq.config) so that it has at least the following entry to allow the default guest account over the network:

```
[
  {rabbit, [{loopback_users, []}]}
].
```

Start RabbitMQ manually, as shown in the following line of code (keep in mind that the server scripts might not be in your $PATH environment as they are usually stored under /usr/local/sbin):

```
$ sudo rabbitmq-server
```

Also, in this case, sudo will ask for our Unix user password in order to proceed. For our examples, we will not configure the broker any further and will simply use its default guest account.

 Interested readers are invited to read the RabbitMQ administration guide available at http://www.rabbitmq.com/admin-guide.html.

At this point, we have everything we need, and we are ready to use Celery. There is an extra dependency that we should really consider installing, even though it is not strictly needed, especially if we just want to play with Celery for the time being. It is the result backend, that is, the special queue that Celery workers use to store the results of their computations. The recommended result store is **Redis** (`http://redis.io`). This step is optional but highly recommended and, just like in the case of RabbitMQ, it needs to be performed on just one machine, say HOST2.

Installing Redis is very simple, as binaries exist for most Linux distribution as well as Mac OS X and Windows. We will install Redis on our Mac machine using homebrew, as follows:

```
$ brew install redis
```

On other operating systems such as Linux, we can simply install the official binaries (for example, `sudo apt-get install redis-server` on Ubuntu Linux).

We can start the database server very easily, as shown in the following command:

```
$ sudo redis-server
```

The rest of the chapter will assume the presence of a dedicated result backend and will point out the difference in configuration and/or code necessary in case a result backend is not available. At the same time, however, anybody seriously considering using Celery in production should consider using a result backend.

Testing the installation

Let's try a quick example to make sure that our Celery installation is working. We will need four terminal windows on, ideally, three different machines (again, we will call them HOST1, HOST2, HOST3, and HOST4). We will start RabbitMQ in one window on HOST1, as shown in the following command (make sure that you use the correct path to `rabbitmq-server`):

```
HOST1 $ sudo /usr/local/sbin/rabbitmq-server
```

In another terminal window (on HOST2), start Redis (if you did not install it, skip to the next paragraph) as follows (make sure to use the correct path to `redis-server`):

```
HOST2 $ sudo /usr/local/bin/redis-server
```

Finally, in a third window (HOST3), create the following Python script (always remember to activate our virtual environment using workon book) and call it test.py:

```
import celery

app = celery.Celery('test',
                        broker='amqp://HOST1',
                        backend='redis://HOST2')



@app.task
def echo(message):
    return message
```

What this code does is pretty simple; it imports the Celery package and defines a Celery application (app in the preceding code) called test, the same as the script where it is defined (this is standard practice for Celery). The application is configured to use the default account and message queue on the RabbitMQ broker running on HOST1 and the default Redis database on HOST2.

In order to use RabbitMQ as the result backend instead of Redis, one would need to make a small edit in the preceding script, replacing the backend endpoint as shown in the following commands:

```
import celery

app = celery.Celery('test',
                        broker='amqp://HOST1',
                        backend=amqp://HOST1')



@app.task
def echo(message):
    return message
```

Once we have an application instance, we use it to decorate the functions we want to make available to our remote workers (using the @app.task decorator). In our case, we decorate a simple function that returns whatever message is passed to it (echo).

With this setup in place, we can simply start a pool of remote workers in the terminal on HOST3, as shown in this command:

```
HOST3 $ celery -A test worker --loglevel=info
```

Just remember to be in the same directory as `test.py` (or point the PYTHONPATH environment variable to the directory where `test.py` lives) so that Celery is able to import our code.

The `celery` command will start, by default, as many worker processes as there are CPUs/cores in our machine. Workers will use the application called `app` in the `test` module (we could use the fully qualified Celery instance name as in `celery -A test.app worker`) and will use the INFO logging level to print log messages to the console. On my laptop (a quad-core machine with **HyperThreading**), Celery starts eight-worker processes by default.

In the fourth terminal window (on HOST4), copy the `test.py` script, activate the `book` virtual environment (that is, via `workon book`), and then start a Python interpreter in the same directory where `test.py` is, as shown in the following commands:

```
HOST4 $ python3.5
Python 3.5.0 (v3.5.0:374f501f4567, Sep 12 2015, 11:00:19)
[GCC 4.2.1 (Apple Inc. build 5666) (dot 3)] on darwin
Type "help", "copyright", "credits" or "license" for more information.
```

Import our `echo` function from the `test` module we just copied over from HOST3, as shown here:

```
>>> from test import echo
```

We can now call `echo` as a normal Python function. In this case, `echo` will run on the local host (that is, HOST4) directly in the interpreter, as shown in the following commands:

```
>>> res = echo('Python rocks!')
>>> print(res)
Python rocks!
```

In order to ask our worker processes on HOST3 to run the `echo()` function, we cannot call the function directly as we did in the previous section. Instead, we need to call its `delay` method (injected by the `@app.task` decorator), as shown in these commands:

```
>>> res = echo.delay('Python rocks!'); print(type(res)); print(res)
<class 'celery.result.AsyncResult'>
1423ec2b-b6c7-4c16-8769-e62e09c1fced
>>> res.ready()
True
>>> res.result
'Python rocks!'
```

As we can see from the preceding Python session, calling `echo.delay('Python rocks!')` does not return a string. Instead, it puts a request to execute the `echo` function in the task queue (running on `HOST1` in the RabbitMQ server) and returns a Future or, more precisely, an `AsyncResult` (Celery's flavor of Future) instance. Just as we saw with the `concurrent.futures` module, this object is simply a placeholder for data that is going to be produced by an asynchronous call. In our case, the asynchronous call is our `echo` function that we inserted in the task queue and has been picked up by a Celery worker somewhere (`HOST3` in our simple case).

We can query `AsyncResult` objects to know whether or not they are ready. If so, we can access their result property, which in our case will simply be the `'Python rocks!'` string.

Switching to the terminal window where we started the worker processes, we can see that the worker pool indeed received our request to work on the `echo` task, as the following logs show:

```
[2015-11-10 08:30:12,869: INFO/MainProcess] Received task: test.
echo[1423ec2b-b6c7-4c16-8769-e62e09c1fced]
```

```
[2015-11-10 08:30:12,886: INFO/MainProcess] Task test.echo[1423ec2b-
b6c7-4c16-8769-e62e09c1fced] succeeded in 0.01469148206524551s: 'Python
rocks!'
```

We can now quit the interpreter and the worker processes (by simply using *CTRL* + *C* in the terminal window where we issue the `celery worker` command): our Celery installation works.

A tour of Celery

What is a distributed task queue and how does Celery implement one? It turns out that distributed task queues are a type of architecture that has been around for quite some time. They are a form of master-worker architecture with a middleware layer that uses a set of queues for work requests (that is, the task queues) and a queue, or a storage area, to hold the results (that is, the result backend).

The master process (also called a **client** or **producer**) puts work requests (that is, tasks) into one of the task queues and fetches results from the result backend. Worker processes, on the other hand, subscribe to some or all of the task queues to know what work to perform and put their results (if any) into the result backend.

This is a very simple and flexible architecture. Master processes do not need to know how many workers are available nor on which machines they are running. They just need to know where the queues are and how to post a request for work.

The same can be said for the worker processes; they do not need to know anything about where the work requests come from and what further processing is to be done with the results that they generate. All they need to know is where to fetch work from and where to store results.

The beauty of this is that the number, type, and morphology of the workers processes can change at any time without affecting the functionality of the system (it will, however, most likely affect its performance and latency). Distributed task queues are easy to scale (just add more workers) and prioritize (define queues with different priorities and attach different numbers of workers to different queues).

Another attractive aspect of such a decoupled system is that in principle, workers and producers can be written in different languages. We could have, for instance, Python code generating work that is going to be performed by workers written in C in cases where performance is paramount.

Celery uses third-party, robust, and battle-tested systems for its queues and result backend. The recommended broker is RabbitMQ, which is what we have used in the previous simple test and which is what we are going to use going forward. While RabbitMQ is a very sophisticated message broker with lots of features, we are not really going to explore it much and rather use it as a black box. The same can be said for the result backend, which can be provided by a simple RabbitMQ queue (for very simple installations), or better, by a dedicated service such as Redis.

The following diagram illustrates, schematically, the architecture of a typical Celery application using RabbitMQ and Redis:

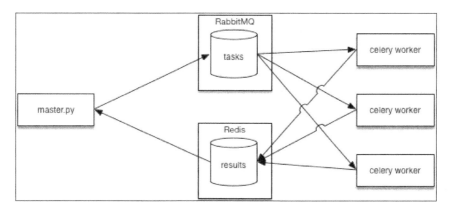

Each of the processes in the rectangular boxes (that is, RabbitMQ, Redis, the workers, and `master.py`) can run on a different machine. Simpler installations will usually host RabbitMQ and Redis on the same host and maybe have just one or two nodes for the workers. Bigger installations will want to use more machines and possibly dedicated servers.

More complex Celery applications

We will implement two simple but interesting applications using Celery. The first one is a reimplementation of the currency exchange rate example from *Chapter 3, Parallelism in Python*, and the second one is a distributed sort algorithm.

We are going to use a total of four machines again (HOST1, HOST2, HOST3, and HOST4) for all these examples. As we did before, machine one (HOST1) will run RabbitMQ. The second machine (HOST2) will run Redis, the third one (HOST3) will run Celery workers, and finally, the fourth one (HOST4) will run our main code.

Let's start with a simple example. Create a new Python script (celery/currency.py) and write the following code (if you're not using Redis, remember to change backend to 'amqp://HOST1'):

```python
import celery
import urllib.request


app = celery.Celery('currency',
                    broker='amqp://HOST1',
                    backend='redis://HOST2')


URL = 'http://finance.yahoo.com/d/quotes.csv?s={}=X&f=p'

@app.task
def get_rate(pair, url_tmplt=URL):
    with urllib.request.urlopen(url_tmplt.format(pair)) as res:
        body = res.read()
    return (pair, float(body.strip()))


if __name__ == '__main__':
    import argparse

    parser = argparse.ArgumentParser()
    parser.add_argument('pairs', type=str, nargs='+')
```

```
    args = parser.parse_args()

    results = [get_rate.delay(pair) for pair in args.pairs]
    for result in results:
        pair, rate = result.get()
        print(pair, rate)
```

The preceding commands are almost identical to the thread version we saw in *Chapter 3, Parallelism in Python*. The main difference is that since we are using Celery, we do not need to create queues; Celery does that for us behind the scenes. In addition, instead of spawning one thread per currency pair, we simply let our Celery workers take care of fetching the work requests from the queue, executing the corresponding function calls, and once this is done, returning the results.

It is instructive to explore a few possible behaviors, such as a successful call, a call that is not worked on because of lack of workers, and a call that fails and raises an exception. Let's start with the straightforward case where everything works.

As we did in the simple `echo` application, let's start (unless they are already running) RabbitMQ and Redis on their respective host(s) (again, via the `redis-server` and `rabbitmq-server` command-line tools).

Then, on the worker host (`HOST3`), copy the `currency.py` script over, change cd to its directory, and start a pool of Celery workers (remember that by default, Celery starts as many worker processes as there are CPU cores), as shown in the following command:

```
HOST3 $ celery -A currency worker --loglevel=info
```

Finally, copy the same script over to `HOST4` and run it as follows:

```
HOST4 $ python3.5 currency.py EURUSD CHFUSD GBPUSD GBPEUR CADUSD CADEUR
EURUSD 1.0644
CHFUSD 0.986
GBPUSD 1.5216
GBPEUR 1.4296
CADUSD 0.751
CADEUR 0.7056
```

Everything worked just fine and we got our five exchange rates back. If we look at the terminal where we started the worker pool (`HOST3`), we will see some log entries similar to the ones shown in the following screenshot:

These are the default log entries that Celery workers emit at `loglevel=info`. Each task is assigned a unique ID (for example, `f8658917-868c-4eb5-b744-6aff997c6dd2` for the task fetching the GBP versus USD rate), and basic timing information is printed for each of them in addition to their return values.

What would happen if there were no workers available? The simple way to find out is to stop the workers (via *CTRL + C* in their terminal window) and rerun `currency.py` on `HOST4`, as shown in this command:

```
HOST4 $ python3.5 currency.py EURUSD CHFUSD GBPUSD GBPEUR CADUSD CADEUR
```

Nothing happens, and `currency.py` hangs around waiting for some workers to come online and perform the work. This behavior might or might not be what we want; on one hand, it sure is convenient to have our script wait for workers to become available without crashing. On the other hand, we might want to give up waiting after a while. One way of doing this is to use the optional `timeout` argument in `result.get()`.

For instance, modifying the code to use `result.get(timeout=1)` would result in the following output (still in the absence of workers):

```
HOST4 $ python3.5 currency.py EURUSD CHFUSD GBPUSD GBPEUR CADUSD CADEUR
 Traceback (most recent call last):
  File "currency.py", line 29, in <module>
    pair, rate = result.get(timeout=1)
  File "/venvs/book/lib/python3.5/site-packages/celery/result.py", line
169, in get
    no_ack=no_ack,
  File " /venvs/book/lib/python3.5/site-packages/celery/backends/base.
py", line 226, in wait_for
    raise TimeoutError('The operation timed out.')
celery.exceptions.TimeoutError: The operation timed out.
```

Of course, we should always use timeouts and catch the corresponding exceptions as part of our error handling strategy.

One interesting point to keep in mind is that, by default, task queues are persistent and their entries do not expire (Celery allows us to configure things differently if we choose to). This means that, if we started some workers now, they would start fetching pending tasks from the queue and return exchange rates. We can clean the queue using the `celery` command-line tool as follows:

```
HOST4 $ celery purge
WARNING: This will remove all tasks from queue: celery.
         There is no undo for this operation!


(to skip this prompt use the -f option)


Are you sure you want to delete all tasks (yes/NO)? yes
Purged 12 messages from 1 known task queue.
```

Let's now see what happens if, for some reason, our tasks generate an exception. Modify the `currency.py` script (on HOST3 at the very least) so that `get_rate` throws an exception, as follows:

```
@app.task
def get_rate(pair, url_tmplt=URL):
    raise Exception('Booo!')
```

Now, restart the pool of workers on HOST3 (that is, HOST3 $ celery -A currency worker --loglevel=info), and then start the main program on HOST4 as follows:

```
HOST4 $ python3.5 currency.py EURUSD CHFUSD GBPUSD GBPEUR CADUSD CADEUR
Traceback (most recent call last):
  File "currency.py", line 31, in <module>
    pair, rate = result.get(timeout=1)
  File "/Users/fpierfed/Documents/venvs/book/lib/python3.5/site-packages/
celery/result.py", line 175, in get
    raise meta['result']
Exception: Booo!
```

What just happened is that all our workers raised exceptions that got propagated to the calling code and returned to us at the first call to `result.get()`.

We should be careful to catch any exceptions that our tasks might raise. We need to keep in mind that code that runs remotely might fail for a number of reasons not necessarily related to the code itself, and we need to be able to react gracefully in those cases.

Celery helps us in a number of ways; as we saw, we can use timeouts to fetch results. We can have failed tasks be resubmitted automatically (refer to the `retry` parameter in the `task` decorator). We can also expire requests for work (refer to the `expires` parameter in a task's `apply_async` method, which is just a more powerful variant of `delay` that we used so far).

Sometimes, we have more complex task graphs than we have seen so far. In these cases, the result of one or more tasks needs to be fed to another task. Celery has support for sophisticated calling patterns that, it should be noted, come with some important performance penalties.

To investigate these, let's implement our second example: a distributed merge sort algorithm. This is going to be a longer code example split into two files: one for the algorithm itself (`mergesory.py`) and one for the main code (`main.py`).

Mergesort is a simple algorithm based on the idea of recursively splitting an input list in half, sorting the two halves, and then merging the results together. Create a new Python script (`celery/mergesort.py`) with the following code:

```python
import celery


app = celery.Celery('mergesort',
                    broker='amqp://HOST1',
                    backend='redis://HOST2')


@app.task
def sort(xs):
    lenxs = len(xs)
    if(lenxs <= 1):
        return(xs)

    half_lenxs = lenxs // 2
    left = xs[:half_lenxs]
```

```
        right = xs[half_lenxs:]
        return(merge(sort(left), sort(right)))



def merge(left, right):
    nleft = len(left)
    nright = len(right)

    merged = []
    i = 0
    j = 0
    while i < nleft and j < nright:
        if(left[i] < right[j]):
            merged.append(left[i])
            i += 1
        else:
            merged.append(right[j])
            j += 1
    return merged + left[i:] + right[j:]
```

The code should be pretty straightforward; we start off by defining our Celery application object app, which uses RabbitMQ for the task queue and Redis for the result backend. Then, we define our sort algorithm, which uses the ancillary merge function to combine the two (sorted) sublists into a single sorted list.

Now, for the main code, create a second script (celery/main.py) with the following commands:

```
#!/usr/bin/env python3.5
import random
import time
from celery import group
from mergesort import sort, merge



# Create a list of 1,000,000 elements in random order.
sequence = list(range(1000000))
```

```
random.shuffle(sequence)


t0 = time.time()


# Split the sequence in a number of chunks and process those
# independently.
n = 4
l = len(sequence) // n
subseqs = [sequence[i * l:(i + 1) * l] for i in range(n - 1)]
subseqs.append(sequence[(n - 1) * l:])


# Ask the Celery workers to sort each sub-sequence.
# Use a group to run the individual independent tasks as a unit of work.
partials = group(sort.s(seq) for seq in subseqs)().get()


# Merge all the individual sorted sub-lists into our final result.
result = partials[0]
for partial in partials[1:]:
    result = merge(result, partial)


dt = time.time() - t0
print('Distributed mergesort took %.02fs' % (dt))


# Do the same thing locally and compare the times.
t0 = time.time()
truth = sort(sequence)
dt = time.time() - t0
print('Local mergesort took %.02fs' % (dt))


# Final sanity checks.
assert result == truth
assert result == sorted(sequence)
```

As the comments in the code suggest, we first generate a suitably large sequence of integers (`sequence = list(range(1000000))`) in a random order (this is what `random.shuffle` does). Then, we split it into a small number (n=4) of sublists of approximately the same length.

Once we have the sublists, we can process them in parallel (assuming, of course, that we have more than n=4 workers available). The main trouble though is that we would like to be notified somehow when these lists have been sorted so that we can merge them back into our final sorted list.

Celery offers a number of primitives to orchestrate task execution, and group is one of them. It allows the execution of concurrent tasks by bundling them, conceptually, in a virtual task. The return value of group is GroupResult (part of the same class hierarchy as AsyncResult). The GroupResult get() method necessary in case a result backend is not available. until all the tasks in the group are done and returns their results in a list. The group callable method takes a list of task signatures (which is what you get by calling a task s() method with the arguments to the task, for example, sort.s(seq) in the preceding code). Task signatures are the mechanism that Celery uses to pass tasks as arguments to other tasks without executing them on the spot.

The rest of the code just merges the sorted sublists locally, two at a time. After the distributed sort, we then re-sort the original list locally using the same algorithm, and compare the results. At the end of the script, we compare the merge-sort results with the built-in sorted call.

To run the example, we need to start RabbitMQ and Redis if they are not running already. Then, we need to start some workers on HOST3, as follows:

```
HOST3 $ celery -A mergesort worker --loglevel=info
```

Just remember to copy mergesort.py over and to change position yourself in the same directory (or define PYTHONPATH to point out to the directory where mergesort.py lives).

After that, we can run the example on HOST4, as follows:

```
HOST4 $ python3.5 main.py
Distributed mergesort took 10.84s
Local mergesort took 26.18s
```

Looking at the Celery logs, we see the n tasks being received and worked on by the worker pool and the results being sent back to the caller.

Performance is definitely not what we were expecting. A simple implementation using multiple processes (either using multiprocessing or concurrent.futures) shows that we can expect almost n-fold performance gain with this simple algorithm (seven seconds using four workers).

The main issue here is that Celery synchronization primitives are quite expensive and should only be used when absolutely necessary. The main reason for this is that Celery keeps polling for the partial results from a group to be ready so that subsequent tasks can be scheduled. This very polling can introduce significant overheads.

Celery in production

Here are some helpful tips on how to run a large Celery application in a production environment.

The first suggestion is to use a configuration module for your Celery application rather than configuring the Celery app in your worker code. Assuming that your configuration file is called `config.py`, you can pass it to a Celery application as follows:

```
import celery

app = celery.Celery('mergesort')

app.config_from_object('config')
```

Then, together with any other configuration directive that might be relevant to the specific application being developed, put the following code in `config.py`:

```
BROKER_URL = 'amqp://HOST1'

CELERY_RESULT_BACKEND = 'redis://HOST2'
```

Probably, the main performance-related suggestion would be to use more than one queue so that tasks can be prioritized and/or separated based on their expected runtime. Using multiple queues and routing tasks to the appropriate queue is a simple way to assign more horsepower (that is, workers) to one group of tasks. Celery provides sophisticated ways to route tasks to queues. Setting this up is a two-step process; first, configure your Celery application and then start the appropriate workers, as the following snippets show:

```
# In config.py

CELERY_ROUTES = {project.task1': {'queue': 'queue1'},
                 'project.task2': {'queue': 'queue2'}}
```

To start some workers on the queues, use the following code, potentially on different machines:

```
HOST3 $ celery -A project worker -Q queue1

HOST5 $ celery -A project worker -Q queue2
```

Using the Celery command-line tool's `-c` flag, one can control the worker pool size, for example, to start a pool of eight workers:

```
HOST3 $ celery -A project worker -c 8
```

Talking about workers, one should notice that, by default, Celery will start a pool of worker processes using the multiprocessing module. This means that each worker will be a full Python process. If some workers exclusively handle I/O intensive tasks, then it could be worthwhile to switch from a multiprocessing-based concurrency to coroutines or threads, as we saw in previous chapters. This can be accomplished using the `-P` flag, as shown in the following command:

```
$ celery -A project worker -P threads
```

Using threads or coroutines for workers could save resources but would have disastrous effects on CPU-bound tasks, as we saw in the previous chapter (the Fibonacci example).

Speaking of performance, one should try and avoid synchronization primitives (like the `group()` function that we saw in the preceding section) unless absolutely needed. In cases where synchronization is unavoidable, a good idea is to try to use a result backend (such as Redis) that has native support for them. In addition, if possible, one should avoid passing complex objects to remote tasks, since these objects would need to be serialized and deserialized, which is usually expensive.

In addition, if the result of a task is not needed, one should make sure to tell Celery not to fetch these results. This is accomplished using the `@task(ignore_result=True)` decorator. If the results from *all* tasks are ignored, then one can avoid defining a result backend. The resulting performance boost will be significant.

Apart from all of these, which are indeed important points, the main decisions to make will be how to start the workers, where to run them, and how to make sure that they keep running. The default answer to these questions is to use a tool such as **supervisord** (`http://supervisord.org`) to manage worker processes.

Celery ships with an example configuration for supervisord (in the `extra/supervisord` directory of the source distribution). For monitoring, a good general solution is **flower** (`https://github.com/mher/flower`), a web-based control and monitoring tool for Celery workers.

Finally, careful consideration should be given to both the broker and the result backend. RabbitMQ and Redis are a good combination that will probably just work for most projects.

Celery alternatives – Python-RQ

A lightweight and simpler alternative to Celery is Python-RQ (http://python-rq.org). It is based on Redis alone as a provider of both task queue and result backend. It is intended for those applications where complex task dependencies or task routing is not necessary.

Since Celery and Python-RQ are conceptually very similar, let's jump right in and rewrite one of our earlier examples. Create a new Python script (rq/currency.py) with the following command:

```
import urllib.request


URL = 'http://finance.yahoo.com/d/quotes.csv?s={}=X&f=p'


def get_rate(pair, url_tmplt=URL):
    # raise Exception('Booo!')

    with urllib.request.urlopen(url_tmplt.format(pair)) as res:
        body = res.read()
    return (pair, float(body.strip()))
```

This is simply the same code from all the currency examples that we saw so far—nothing new here. The main difference with the Celery implementation is that this code has no dependency on Python-RQ or Redis. Copy this script to the worker node (HOST3).

The main program is going to be similarly simple. Create a new Python script (rq/main.py) using the following code:

```
#!/usr/bin/env python3
import argparse
import redis
import rq
from currency import get_rate


parser = argparse.ArgumentParser()
```

```
parser.add_argument('pairs', type=str, nargs='+')
args = parser.parse_args()


conn = redis.Redis(host='HOST2')
queue = rq.Queue(connection=conn)


jobs = [queue.enqueue(get_rate, pair) for pair in args.pairs]


for job in jobs:
    while job.result is None:
        pass
    print(*job.result)
```

This is where we see Python-RQ in action. We need to connect to our Redis server (running on HOST2) explicitly and then pass the newly created connection object to the Queue class constructor. The resulting Queue object is what we will use to submit our work requests. This is done by passing the function object and any arguments to queue.enqueue.

The result of enqueueing a function call is a job instance, which is the same asynchronous call placeholder that we have seen many times with many different names.

Since Python-RQ does not have Celery's blocking AsyncResult.get() method, we have to implement a little event loop ourselves and keep polling the job instances to check whether their result property is not None (which would mean that they position yourself in). This pattern is not really recommended in production code, as one would end up over polling, wasting resources, or under polling, wasting time, but it will be fine for this silly example.

In order to run the example, we first need to install Python-RQ, which is easily accomplished using pip, as the following command demonstrates:

```
$ pip install rq
```

We will need to do this on all machines where we will be running either the main code or workers. Then, on HOST2, start Redis, as always:

```
$ sudo redis-server
```

On the worker nodes (HOST3 in our case), start some workers. Python-RQ does not automatically start a pool of workers for us. One simple way to start more than one worker that will suffice for now is to use a script like the following one (start_workers.py):

```
#!/usr/bin/env python3
import argparse
import subprocess


def terminate(proc, timeout=.5):
    """

    Perform a two-step termination of process `proc`: send a SIGTERM

    and, after `timeout` seconds, send a SIGKILL. This should give

    `proc` enough time to do any necessary cleanup.

    """

    if proc.poll() is None:
        proc.terminate()
        try:
            proc.wait(timeout)
        except subprocess.TimeoutExpired:
            proc.kill()
    return


parser = argparse.ArgumentParser()
parser.add_argument('N', type=int)
args = parser.parse_args()


workers = []
for _ in range(args.N):
    workers.append(subprocess.Popen(['rqworker',
                                      '-u', 'redis://yippy']))
try:
    running = [w for w in workers if w.poll() is None]
    while running:
        proc = running.pop(0)
```

```
        try:
            proc.wait(timeout=1.)
        except subprocess.TimeoutExpired:
            running.append(proc)
except KeyboardInterrupt:
    for w in workers:
        terminate(w)
```

This script will start a user-supplied number of Python-RQ worker processes (by using the `rqworker` script, part of the Python-RQ distribution) and kill them gracefully on *Ctrl + C*. A more robust way to start our workers would be to use something like supervisord, which we briefly mentioned in the preceding section.

Run the preceding script on HOST3 as follows:

```
HOST3 $ ./start_workers.py 6
```

We can now run the code. On HOST4, run `main.py` as follows:

```
HOST4 $ python3.5 main.py EURUSD CHFUSD GBPUSD GBPEUR CADUSD CADEUR
EURUSD 1.0635
CHFUSD 0.9819
GBPUSD 1.5123
GBPEUR 1.422
CADUSD 0.7484
CADEUR 0.7037
```

The behavior is the same as Celery's.

Celery alternatives – Pyro

Pyro (`http://pythonhosted.org/Pyro4/`), which stands for Python Remote Objects, is a package that has been around for quite some time, since 1998 or so. As a result, it is remarkably stable and feature-complete.

It takes a very different approach to task distribution than Celery or Python-RQ in that it exposes Python objects as servers on a network. It then creates proxy objects to them so that the calling code sees them as local objects. This architecture was very popular at the end of the 90s with systems such as CORBA and Java RMI.

The fact that Pyro is somewhat hiding the fact that some of the objects in one's code are local and some are remote is at times a source of criticism. The reason being that there are a number of failure modes intrinsic to running remote code that are easy to forget when remote code execution is hidden behind a proxy object.

Another source of criticism is that Pyro can be somewhat difficult to get running correctly on an ad hoc network, where not all hostnames can be resolved, or in networks where UDP broadcasting is disabled.

Despite all of this, most developers find Pyro to be very simple to use and extremely robust in production.

Its installation is simple, as Pyro is a pure Python module with few dependencies. It can be installed with `pip`, as we have done so far with all other modules, as follows:

```
$ pip install pyro4
```

The `pip` command will install Pyro version 4.x as well as Serpent, the serializer that Pyro uses behind the scenes to encode and decode Python objects.

Rewriting the previous currency exchange rate application using Pyro will be only a tiny bit more complex than with Python-RQ, and it will involve one extra piece of software: the Pyro nameserver. We will, however, not need any broker or result backend as all Pyro objects will communicate directly with each other.

The high-level description of how Pyro works is as follows. Every object that we choose to access remotely is wrapped by the framework in a socket server listening for connections. Once some piece of code calls a method on one such remote object, the method call, together with its parameters, is serialized and sent over the wire to the appropriate object/server. At this point, the remote object performs whatever actions have been requested and sends the results back over the same connection (again, transparently serialized) to the calling code.

Since each remote object can itself call any other remote object, this architecture can be quite decentralized. In addition, once established, communication between objects is peer to peer, which is radically different from the loosely coupled architecture of distributed task queues. Another interesting aspect of Pyro applications is that each remote object can function as both a master and a worker.

Let's rewrite the currency exchange rate application using Pyro so that we can see how the code performs under a different architecture. Starting from the currency example, create a new Python script (`pyro/worker.py`) with the following code:

```
import urllib.request
```

```
import Pyro4


URL = 'http://finance.yahoo.com/d/quotes.csv?s={}=X&f=p'


@Pyro4.expose(instance_mode="percall")
class Worker(object):
    def get_rate(self, pair, url_tmplt=URL):
        with urllib.request.urlopen(url_tmplt.format(pair)) as res:
            body = res.read()
        return (pair, float(body.strip()))



# Create a Pyro daemon which will run our code.
daemon = Pyro4.Daemon()
uri = daemon.register(Worker)
Pyro4.locateNS().register('MyWorker', uri)


# Sit in an infinite loop accepting connections
print('Accepting connections')
try:
    daemon.requestLoop()
except KeyboardInterrupt:
    daemon.shutdown()
print('All done')
```

The worker code starts off quite similar to what we have seen so far, with the only slight difference that we have turned the `get_rate` function into a method of the `Worker` class. The reason behind this change is that Pyro allows us to export class instances, not simple functions.

The rest of the code is new and specific to Pyro. We need to create a `Daemon` instance (which is essentially a network server behind the scenes) that will take our classes and publish them on the network so that other code can call their methods. This is done in two steps: first, create an instance of the `Pyro4.Daemon` class and then add classes to it by passing them to its `register` method.

Each Pyro `Daemon` instance can shadow any number of classes exposing their functionality over the network. Internally, the `Daemon` object will create instances of the classes it shadows, on an as-needed basis (which means that if no code ever uses a class, the corresponding `Daemon` object will not instantiate it).

By default, `Daemon` objects instantiate their registered classes once per network connection, which is not what we want if we are to perform actions concurrently. The default behavior can be changed by decorating the registered classes with `@Pyro4.expose(instance_mode=...)`.

The supported values for `instance_mode` are three: `single`, `session`, and `percall`. Using `single` means that `Daemon` will create one instance of our class and use it for all requests across clients. The same can be achieved by registering an instance of the class (rather than the class itself).

Using `session` gives us the default behavior: each client connection gets a new instance that is used for all method invocations by that client. Using `instance_mode="percall"`, a new class instance is created for every remote method call.

Regardless of the instance creation mode, registering a class (or instance thereof) with `Daemon` object returns a unique identifier (that is a URI) that other code can use to connect to that object. We could pass that URI around manually, but it is more convenient to store it in the Pyro nameserver, which is achieved in two steps. First, find the nameserver and then register the URI with a name. In the preceding code, this is done in one line:

```
Pyro4.locateNS().register('MyWorker', uri)
```

The nameserver works a bit like a Python dictionary; registering two URIs with the same name results in the second one overwriting the first. In addition, as we will see, client code gets a hold of remote objects using the names stored in the nameserver. This means that particular care should be taken in choosing good names and a good naming strategy, especially when multiple worker processes provide the same functionality.

Finally in the preceding code, we enter the `Daemon` event loop with `daemon.requestLoop()`. The `Daemon` object will sit in an infinite loop servicing client requests.

For the client, create a new Python script (`pyro/main.py`) with the following code:

```
#!/usr/bin/env python3
import argparse
import time
```

```
import Pyro4


parser = argparse.ArgumentParser()
parser.add_argument('pairs', type=str, nargs='+')
args = parser.parse_args()


# Retrieve the rates sequentially.
t0 = time.time()
worker = Pyro4.Proxy("PYRONAME:MyWorker")

for pair in args.pairs:
    print(worker.get_rate(pair))
print('Sync calls: %.02f seconds' % (time.time() - t0))

# Retrieve the rates concurrently.
t0 = time.time()
worker = Pyro4.Proxy("PYRONAME:MyWorker")
async_worker = Pyro4.async(worker)

results = [async_worker.get_rate(pair) for pair in args.pairs]
for result in results:
    print(result.value)
print('Async calls: %.02f seconds' % (time.time() - t0))
```

As you can see, the client performs the same work twice. The reason for that is to show the two interfaces that Pyro offers to remote objects: synchronous and asynchronous method calls.

Looking at the code, we see that we start by getting currency pairs from the command line using the argparse package, as usual. Then, for the synchronous case, we get a hold of the remote Worker object by the name worker = Pyro4.Proxy("PYRONAME:MyWorker"). The PYRONAME: prefix tells Pyro to loop up the instance name in the nameserver for us. This avoids us from locating the nameserver manually.

Once we have the `worker` object, we can call methods on it as if it were a simple local instance of the `worker` class. This is exactly what we do in the first loop that is reprinted as follows:

```
for pair in args.pairs:
    print(worker.get_rate(pair))
```

At each `worker.get_rate(pair)` invocation, the `Proxy` object uses its persistent connection to the remote `Daemon` object and sends it a request to run `get_rate(pair)`. The `Daemon` object, in our case, will create an instance of the `Worker` class each time and call its `get_rate(pair)` method. The result is serialized and sent back to the client, which will then print it. Each call is synchronous and blocks until completed.

In the second loop, we do the same thing, but using the asynchronous calling style. For that, we need to create a `Proxy` object to the remote class as usual, but then, we wrap it in an asynchronous handler. This is what the following code does:

```
worker = Pyro4.Proxy("PYRONAME:MyWorker")
async_worker = Pyro4.async(worker)
```

We can now use `async_worker` to fetch our exchange rates in the background. Each call to `async_worker.get_rate(pair)` is nonblocking and returns an instance of `Pyro4.futures.FutureResult`, which behaves similarly to a `Future` object from the `concurrent.futures` module. Accessing its `value` property will wait until the corresponding asynchronous call is completed.

In order to run the preceding example, we need three terminal windows on potentially three different machines: one for the nameserver (`HOST1`), one for the `Worker` class and its `Daemon` (`HOST2`), and a third one (`HOST3`) for the client (that is, `main.py`).

On the first terminal, start the nameserver as follows:

```
HOST1 $ pyro4-ns --host 0.0.0.0
Broadcast server running on 0.0.0.0:9091
NS running on 0.0.0.0:9090 (0.0.0.0)
Warning: HMAC key not set. Anyone can connect to this server!
URI = PYRO:Pyro.NameServer@0.0.0.0:9090
```

For simplicity, we bind the nameserver to `0.0.0.0` so that anybody can connect to it. We also do not bother setting up authentication, and therefore, we get a warning about it in the second to last line.

Now that the nameserver is up and running, start the worker in the second terminal as follows:

```
HOST2 $ python3.5 worker.py
Accepting connections
```

With the Daemon object accepting connections, we can now go to the last terminal window and run our client code, as follows:

```
HOST3 $ python3.5 main.py EURUSD CHFUSD GBPUSD GBPEUR CADUSD CADEUR
('EURUSD', 1.093)
('CHFUSD', 1.0058)
('GBPUSD', 1.5141)
('GBPEUR', 1.3852)
('CADUSD', 0.7493)
('CADEUR', 0.6856)
Sync calls: 1.55 seconds
('EURUSD', 1.093)
('CHFUSD', 1.0058)
('GBPUSD', 1.5141)
('GBPEUR', 1.3852)
('CADUSD', 0.7493)
('CADEUR', 0.6856)
Async calls: 0.29 seconds
```

The behavior we get is what we were expecting and what we have seen in all these examples—IO-bound code scales very well, to the point where the asynchronous block is six times faster than the synchronous loop.

At this point, it is worth noting a few things about Pyro and our simple example. The first thing to keep in mind is that Pyro Daemon instances expect to be able to resolve the name of the host where they run. If that is not possible, then they will just accept connections from 127.0.0.1, which means that they will not be reachable remotely (they will, however, be accessible from the same machine). The solution is to bind them to the IP address of the machine they run on, making sure that it is not the loopback address. One way to do this is by using the following Python code to select one viable IP:

```
from socket import gethostname, gethostbyname_ex


ips = [ip for ip in gethostbyname_ex(gethostname())[-1]
        if ip != '127.0.0.1']
ip = ips.pop()
```

Another consideration is this: as a consequence of the "connect directly to the named object" approach that Pyro uses, it is hard to have the same transparent concurrency that Celery or Python-RQ give us by starting more workers. In Pyro, we have to name these workers differently and then explicitly connect to them (by Proxying them) by name. This is why, oftentimes, Pyro clients end up implementing a mini scheduler to distribute work among all active workers.

Another potential pitfall is that the nameserver does not keep track of worker disconnects, and hence, finding an object URI by name does not mean that the corresponding remote `Daemon` object is indeed running. It is good practice to always treat any Pyro call for what it is: a call to a remote server that might or might not succeed.

Keeping these simple concepts in mind, Pyro can be used very successfully to build rather complex networked, distributed applications.

Summary

This was a long chapter! We looked at Celery as a powerful package for writing distributed applications in Python. We then looked at Python-RQ, a lightweight and simpler alternative. Both packages use a distributed task queue architecture, which is a multimachine implementation of the same system that is used to distribute work that we saw in *Chapter 3, Parallelism in Python*.

Pyro was then introduced as an alternative approach to both Celery and Python-RQ. Pyro has a very different philosophy that is firmly rooted in the proxy pattern and **remote-procedure-call** (**RPC**) architecture for distributed systems.

Both approaches have their merits and their strengths, and undoubtedly you will find yourselves preferring one or the other.

The next chapter will look at one way to deploy our distributed applications to the cloud — it is going to be a fascinating read.

5

Python in the Cloud

The previous chapter introduced you to Celery and other tools that we can use to create distributed applications with Python. We explored a couple of different distributed computing architectures: distributed task queues and distributed objects. There is, however, an important theme that we did not cover in any depth so far. It is the deployment of our finished application on multiple machines. This is exactly what this chapter is about.

Here, we will look at **Amazon Web Services** (**AWS**), the leading provider of cloud services, and how to deploy our distributed applications on its infrastructure. Clearly, the cloud is not the only way to deploy applications, and in the next chapter, we will, in fact, look at another way to deploy applications—HPC clusters. However, deploying to AWS or one of its competitors can be an easy and relatively inexpensive way of bringing a complex application to life.

Cloud computing and AWS

AWS is the leading provider of cloud computing; that is to say, it is a collection of Internet-based, on-demand computing and storage services, usually with a pay-as-you-go pricing model.

Being able to access the vast pool of computing resources (real or virtualized) and storage units of a cloud provider, means that an application can scale both horizontally (by adding more machines) and vertically (by choosing more powerful hardware) on demand. The same application can, therefore, run with no or very little downtime while adapting to its user load, by increasing or reducing the resources it uses dynamically (and therefore, its cost per unit of time).

This ease of scaling resources, the ability to tap into the vast resources of a big cloud provider such as Amazon, the high availability of cloud infrastructure, and the low prices of computing and storage resources, can make the cloud a very attractive option for application deployment, even for a small company or an individual.

The two main services that a cloud provider offers are compute nodes and storage services. Often, other services are offered as well, including scalable database servers (both relational and NoSQL stores), caches for web applications, specialized computing frameworks (such as Hadoop/MapReduce), as well as application-level services (such as message queues or e-mail services). All of these services can be dynamically scaled up to meet increased usage loads and then scaled back when the application load is lower.

AWS offers all of the preceding services and many more; however, in this chapter, we will look at its main ones: **Amazon Elastic Compute Cloud (EC2)** to compute nodes, **Amazon Elastic Block Store (EBS)** to store compute node virtual disks, **Amazon Simple Storage Server (S3)** to store application data, and finally (briefly), **Amazon Elastic Beanstalk** for application deployment.

Creating an AWS account

In order to use AWS, one needs to create an account. The first year's usage of a reasonable amount of resources is free of charge; after that, standard charges are applied.

To create an account, you can point the web browser to `https://aws.amazon.com` and click on **Create a Free Account**, as shown in the following screenshot:

The account signup sequence asks for basic contact information, a payment method (it is, unfortunately, not possible to sign up for AWS without a debit or credit card), and some further information.

Once the account is active, you can log in to the administration console, which looks like the following screenshot:

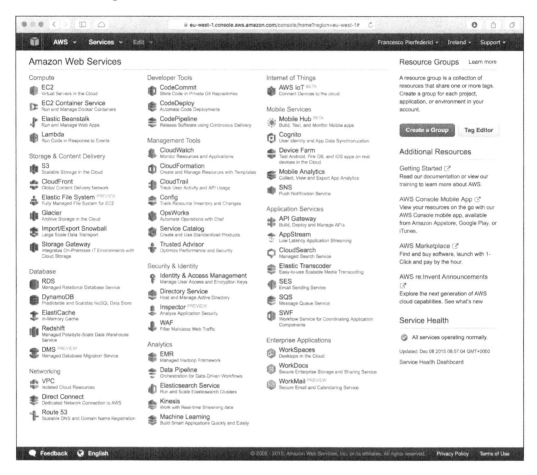

As made apparent by the preceding screenshot, the console page is very busy and has a large number of icons corresponding to more than 50 services that comprise AWS. This chapter will describe how to use **EC2**, **Elastic Beanstalk**, **S3**, and the **Identity and Access Management** service, whose icons are highlighted in the following figure:

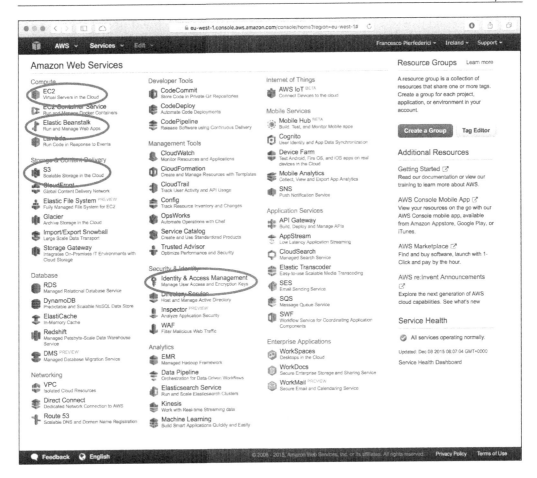

Before we create virtual machines to run our application or storage pods to host our data, we need to create at least one user and one user group. To do that, simply click on the **Identity and Access Management** icon in the second column in the AWS management console, or point the web browser to `https://console.aws.amazon.com/iam/`. Click on **Groups** in the left-hand side pane (the navigation area) and then on the **Create New Group** button in the main pane of the page that opens.

You will be asked to name the new user group. I usually choose `Wheel` as my administration group, but any name will do. After entering the group name, click on **Next Step** at the bottom of the page.

Next, we will be asked to choose which of the several predefined policies we want this user group to have. In this page, we can simply select the one that says **AdministratorAccess**. Click on **Next Step** at the bottom of the page.

Review our choices on the next page and, if everything looks good, you can finally choose **Create Group**. The **Group** page will now list your newly created user group, as shown in the following screenshot:

Clicking on the name of the group (**Wheel** in my case) and then on the **Permissions** tab will reveal the policies associated with that group, as shown in this screenshot:

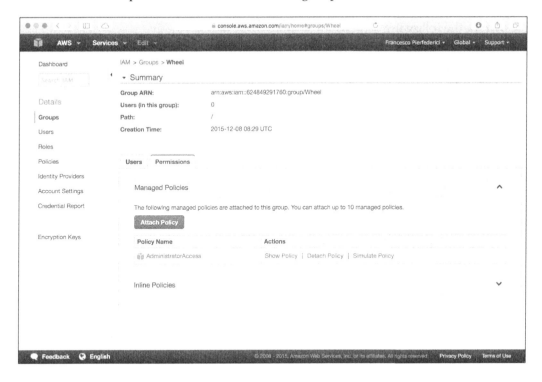

Now, it is time to create at least one user — the one that we will use to log in to our virtual machines. Click on **Users** in the left-hand side pane and then click on **Create New Users** at the top of the page. In the page that opens up, we are able to create up to five user accounts at a time.

Let's just create one for now. Enter the desired username in the first text field (next to the number **1**). Make sure that the **Generate an access key for each user** checkbox is selected and click on the **Create** button at the bottom of the page, as shown in the following screenshot (I chose `bookuser`):

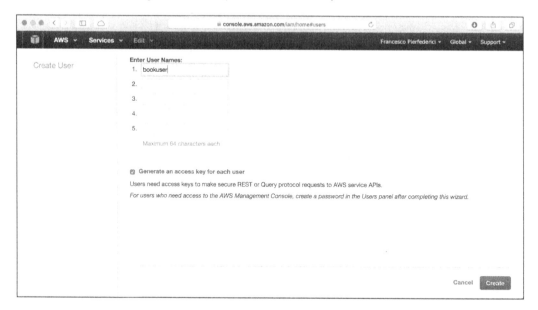

The following page is pretty important; we are presented with a summary of the user creation process together with the ability to download the credentials for our user. Make sure that you click on the **Download Credentials** button at the bottom of the page. If you forget to do that or misplace the credentials file (which is a simple `.csv` file), you can always recreate these credentials later by creating a new user.

Now, we need to add our newly created user to the administrator group. To do that, go back to the **Groups** page (by clicking on **Groups** in the left-hand side navigation pane), select the administrator group we created earlier (Wheel, in my case), click on **Group Actions** at the top of the page, and finally on **Add Users to Group** in the pop-up menu. If that entry appears but it is not enabled, make sure that you have selected the group by clicking on the checkbox next to its name.

We are brought to a new page that lists our user. Click on the checkbox next to the user we just created and then on **Add Users** at the bottom of the page. Clicking on the group name on the next page and then on the **Users** tab should indeed show that your user has been added to your group, as shown in the following screenshot:

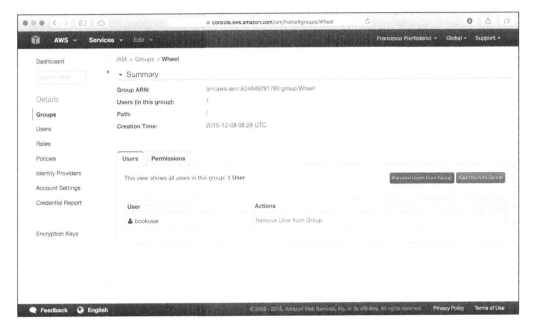

Now, it is time to create a password for our user; go back to the **Users** page (that is, click on **Users** in the left-hand side navigation pane), click on the username, and in the page that opens, click on the **Security Credentials** tab. You will be presented with a page similar to what is shown in the following screenshot:

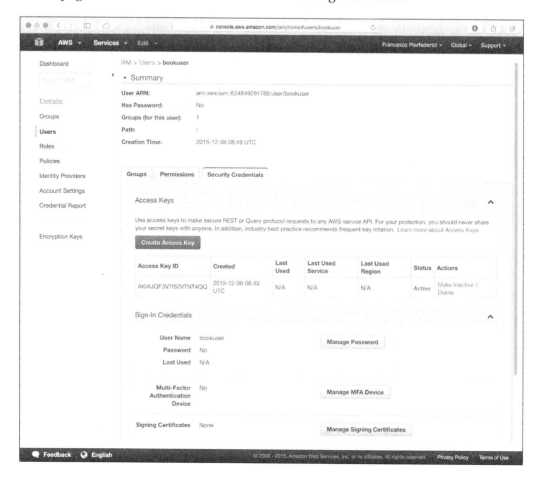

Here, we will create a password for our user by clicking on **Manage Password** under **Sign-In-Credentials** and following the instructions; we can either opt to have AWS create a password for us or enter a custom password ourselves.

We are almost done. What is left to do is create SSH keys for our user so that they can log into our EC2 instances securely without a password. This is accomplished easily using the management console as well.

Log out from the management console and sign back in as the user that we just created. In order to do that, we will use the URL that appears at the top of the page at `https://console.aws.amazon.com/iam`, which has the form `https://<ACCOUNT NUMBER>.signin.aws.amazon.com/console/`.

Now, on the console page, click on the **EC2** icon and select a geographical region for your instances from the pop-up menu at the top left-hand side of the page (**Ireland** in my case). Amazon EC2 virtual machines are organized in a number of different geographical regions, covering the US, Europe, Asia, and South America. SSH keys are specific to a region, meaning that if we want to use machines in two different regions, we will create two SSH key pairs, one for each region.

After choosing the region, click on the **Key Pairs** link in the main pane, as shown in the following screenshot:

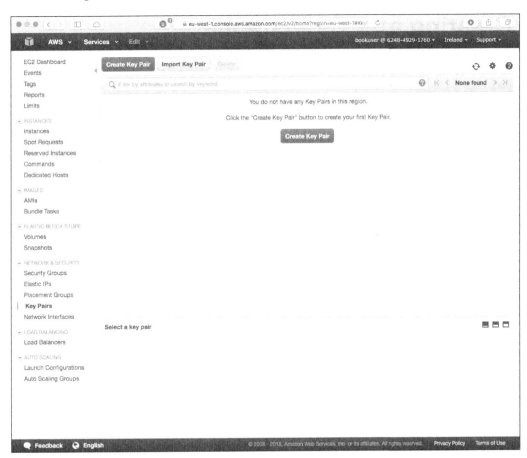

Click on **Create Key Pair**, give it a name that you can remember (bookuser-ireland-key in my case), and click on the **Create** button. The newly created (private) key is automatically downloaded to your computer in the `pem` format (sometimes, the downloaded file will have a `.pem.txt` extension; in that case, we can rename it `.pem`).

Just make sure to store it in a safe place and back it up as we will not be able to download it again. If misplaced, you will need to delete the key-pair using the AWS console and create a new one.

I like to keep my keys in the `.ssh` directory in my `$HOME` location. To this end, I usually copy the key there, rename it so that it has a `.pem` extension, and make sure that it is only accessible by me (that is, `chmod 400 ~/.ssh/bookuser-ireland-key.pem`).

Creating an EC2 instance

After all this setup work, we are now ready to create our first virtual machine; start it in the geographical region of our choice (remember to create a key for every region you choose to use) and log in to the running instance. We will do all of this through the web console for now.

If you are not there already, go back to the AWS web console, log in as our user (remember that you can use `https://<ACCOUNT NUMBER>.signin.aws.amazon.com/console/` URL), and click on the **EC2** icon.

The page that opens up is the EC2 console, as shown in the following screenshot:

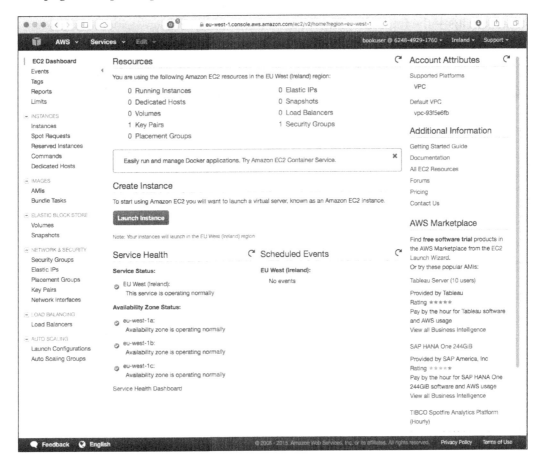

Click on the blue **Launch Instance** button toward the middle of the page, just under the **Create Instance** heading. Now, we will be guided through the process of creating and starting up a virtual machine. First, choose the **Amazon Machine Image** (**AMI**), that is to say, the base operating system and default set of software packages that come with your VM.

There are many possible configurations to choose from. For now, we will restrict ourselves to AMIs that are free tier eligible, running on Linux. I like a 64-bit Ubuntu server image—the fourth one from the top in the following screenshot—but any will do:

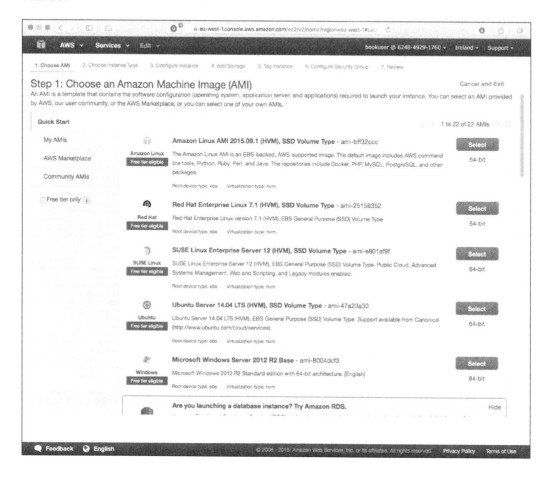

Next, we will choose the virtual hardware of our instance. Amazon offers us several configurations, and the one to choose depends on our intended use. For instance, if we were to run deep learning code, we might want to select an instance type with a beefy GPU. In our case, we will just choose the **Free tier eligible t2.micro** instance: the first one in the following screenshot:

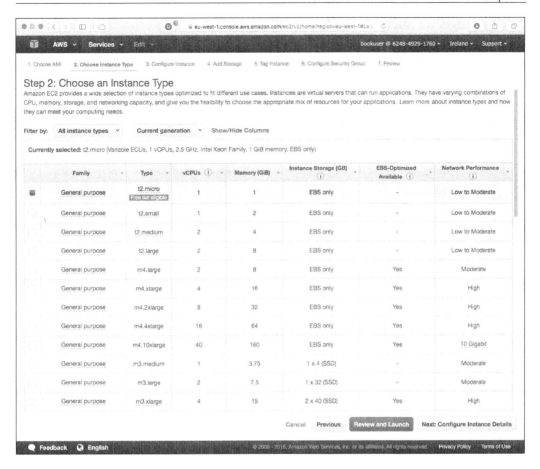

Clicking on **Next: Configure Instance Details** will open a new page where we will be able to configure a few characteristics of the instance we are about to create. For now, we will leave everything at their default values, but we should pay attention to the **Purchasing option** field, which is quite interesting. Here, we have the option of requesting a so-called **Spot instance** option, meaning a VM that will be automatically terminated/suspended if a higher priority instance needs the hardware resources we are using.

We are not going to bother with this option right now, but it is worth keeping it in mind as spot instances are a great way to save money at the cost of having to design our applications so that they gracefully handle interruptions. Click on **Next: Add Storage**.

On this page, we can configure the storage options for our instance. For now, we will leave everything as is, but it is worthwhile to look at the various options offered. Interesting to notice, at this point, is the **Delete on Termination** checkbox, which is selected by default. The consequence of this option is that when we terminate our instances, all data associated with them will be deleted. Since, by default, instances are suspended, not terminated, this is OK for now (more on this later). Next, click on **Next: Tag Instance**. We are not going to create any tags for now, so we will just click on **Next: Configure Security Group**.

The page that opens, which you can see in the following screenshot, is quite important:

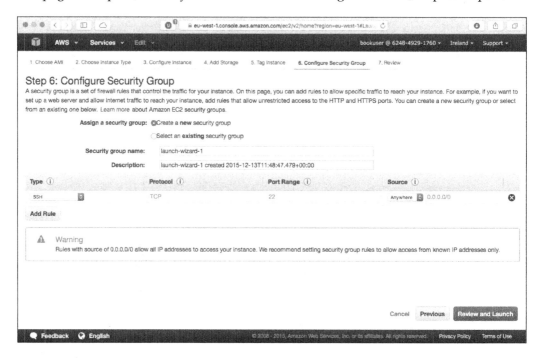

It is on this page, in fact, that we configure which services (that is, which network ports) our instance will open to the outside word and from which set of IP addresses, we will be able to log in to our VM. For now, we will simply change the rule for **SSH** to allow connections from **My IP** (selectable from the pop-up menu under the **Source** heading on the SSH row).

We might decide to open up TCP port 80 to **Anywhere**, for instance, in order to run a web server or TCP port 5672 (the one used by Celery with a RabbitMQ broker) to a selected range of IPs for a Celery application.

For now, we will not create any new rules and be happy with our restricted SSH access rule. The setup should look like the following screenshot:

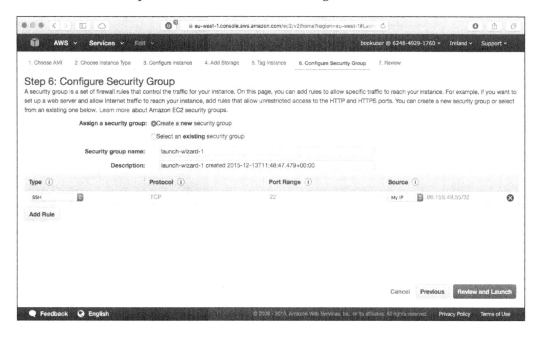

Finally, click on **Review and Launch** and then on **Launch** if you are happy with the choices so far. Make sure that you have access to the right .pem key file to access the EC2 instance, and then, click on **Launch Instances**.

Amazon will now start up our instance (or instances), which can take a few minutes. By clicking on **View Instances** at the bottom of the page, we will be presented with the following page, where we can see our instance running or being prepared:

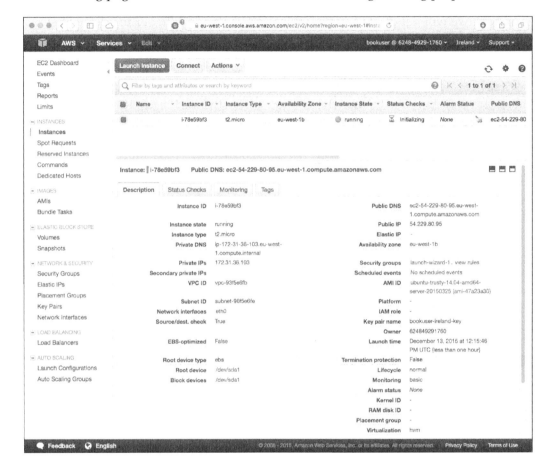

Once our VM runs, we can connect to it using SSH. We will connect to our instance via the terminal, using the appropriate Unix username for the instance OS we have chosen (that is, `ec2-user` for Amazon Linux, `ubuntu` for Ubuntu, either `root` or `ec2-user` for SUSE, and either `fedora` or `ec2-user` for Fedora Linux).

In our case, we will log in as shown in the following screenshot:

As we can see by looking around the running VM, it comes with a number of software packages preinstalled, including Python 2.7 and 3.4. To all practical intents and purposes, this VM is a Linux server that we can administer as normal. Once we are done experimenting, we can stop the instance by selecting **Stop** in the **Actions** pop-up menu, after selecting the instance name, as shown in the following screenshot:

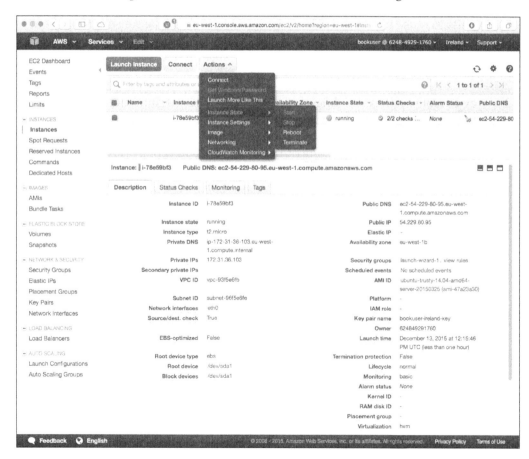

When talking about EC2 instances, one has to pay particular attention to the storage that those virtual machines use and what happens to it once the VM is rebooted, stopped, or terminated. The implications are significant. First of all, regardless of whether we stop or terminate a VM, its IP address is lost and a new one is assigned the next time it runs.

The instance we created (`t2.micro`) uses virtual disks stored on the EBS, which is a high-performance and high-reliability block storage for EC2 instances and, most often, a good choice for an OS disk.

By default, virtual disks stored on EBS are deleted once the corresponding instance is terminated (unless the **Delete on Termination** checkbox is unselected in the **Add Storage** page of the instance creation process that we saw here) but not when it is stopped. The implication is that stopping an instance incurs (outside of the free-tier year) storage costs, whereas terminating an instance (by default) does not.

Restarting a terminated instance is not possible and one has to create a new instance from scratch, which takes longer than restarting a stopped VM. For this reason, if one intends to reuse instances in the short term, it might make sense to stop them rather than terminating them. However, the cost of keeping EBS volumes around is nontrivial, and so, one should terminate the instances that are not going to be used for a while.

One way to have application data persist across restarts/terminations is to create a new EBS volume and, once the relevant EC2 instance is running, attach the new volume to the EC2 instance. This is accomplished by clicking on the **Volumes** link in the right-hand side navigation pane of the **EC2 Dashboard** page (under **ELASTIC BLOCK STORE**) and following the instructions. Just keep in mind that the first time a volume is used, it needs to be formatted, which can be accomplished inside your running EC2 instance using the OS-specific tools, as illustrated in the following screenshot (for our Ubuntu image):

```
ubuntu@ip-172-34-225:~$ lsblk
NAME    MAJ:MIN RM SIZE RO TYPE MOUNTPOINT
xvda    202:0    0  8G  0 disk
`-xvda1 202:1    0  8G  0 part /
xvdf    202:80   0  8G  0 disk
ubuntu@ip-172-34-225:~$ sudo file -s /dev/xvdf
/dev/xvdf: data
ubuntu@ip-172-34-225:~$ sudo mkfs -t ext4 /dev/xvdf
mke2fs 1.42.9 (4-Feb-2014)
Filesystem label=
OS type: Linux
Block size=4096 (log=2)
Fragment size=4096 (log=2)
Stride=0 blocks, Stripe width=0 blocks
524288 inodes, 2097152 blocks
104857 blocks (5.00%) reserved for the super user
First data block=0
Maximum filesystem blocks=2147483648
64 block groups
32768 blocks per group, 32768 fragments per group
8192 inodes per group
Superblock backups stored on blocks:
    32768, 98304, 163840, 229376, 294912, 819200, 884736, 1605632

Allocating group tables: done
Writing inode tables: done
Creating journal (32768 blocks): done
Writing superblocks and filesystem accounting information: done

ubuntu@ip-172-34-225:~$ sudo file -s /dev/xvdf
/dev/xvdf: Linux rev 1.0 ext4 filesystem data, UUID=642f7f14-fb7c-45d7-8922-6dd26e1ad95b (extents) (large files) (huge files)
ubuntu@ip-172-34-225:~$ sudo mkdir /mnt/data
ubuntu@ip-172-34-225:~$ sudo mount /dev/xvdf /mnt/data
ubuntu@ip-172-34-225:~$
```

It is worth noting that the Linux kernel remapped the device name we chose in the EBS volume attach process, /dev/sdf to /dev/xvdf.

Attached volumes behave like hard disks that we connect to a computer; their data persists across reboots and the volumes can be moved from one instance to another. Just remember that we pay for each EBS volume that we create for as long as we keep them around, even if they are not used.

Another (cheaper) option to store application data is to use S3, which is what we will discuss next.

Storing data in Amazon S3

Amazon Simple Storage Service, S3, is a web service that can be used to store and retrieve arbitrary blobs of data. Data stored in S3 can include files of any kind, up to 5 terabytes in size (at the time of writing this), and also raw bytes.

S3 is also significantly cheaper than EBS; however, it does not offer a filesystem layer but rather a REST API. Another difference is that while EBS volumes can only be attached to a single running instance at a time, S3 objects can be shared among as many instances as we want, and depending on the desired permission policy, they can be accessed from anywhere on the Internet.

Getting started with S3 is easy; you need to create a number of buckets (that is, data containers in S3 parlance) in relevant geographical areas (usually, in order to minimize access times) and then add data to them. The process is as follows; if you're not there already, log in to the AWS management console and click on the **S3** icon under **Storage & Content Delivery**. Click on the **Create Bucket** button, give the bucket a name, and choose a geographical region for its storage.

For this example, we will choose **book-123-456** as the name and **Ireland** as the region, as shown in the following screenshot:

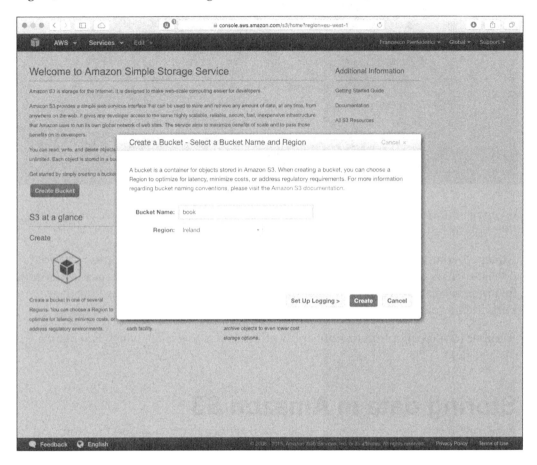

Just click on **Create** and we are done. Since bucket names are shared among all S3 users, one quickly finds out that common names, such as book, are already taken. It is, therefore, easier and less frustrating to use descriptive names and then append some form of unique identifier, just as we did in the preceding example.

The next page to be displayed shows the list of S3 buckets that we have access to. For now, it lists only the bucket that we just created, as shown in the following screenshot (clicking on the icon on the left-hand side of the bucket name displays the bucket properties):

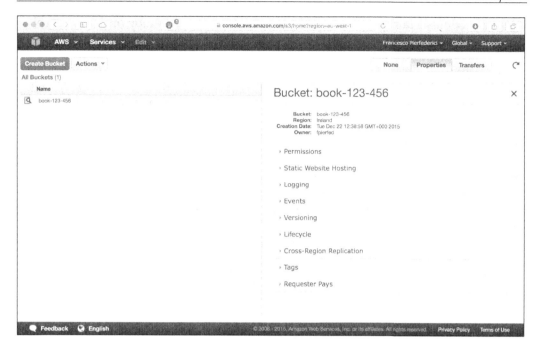

From this page, we can click on the bucket page to list the bucket content (if any), upload data, rename it, or delete it, as shown in the next screenshot:

Amazon S3 has a fairly sophisticated permission system whereby one can control access rights on a per-object and/or per-bucket basis. Let's now upload a simple file to our bucket and see how to change its access permissions so that we can view it from anywhere.

Create a text file with some text in it. In my case, I just created a file called `index.html` with the `"Hi there!"` text in it. Once this is done, upload the file to your S3 bucket using the web interface (that is, click on the bucket name and then on **Upload** in the top-left corner of the page and follow the instructions).

We can inspect the file properties (including permissions) by selecting the file and then clicking on **Properties** in the top-right corner of the bucket page. As we can see from the following screenshot, by default, the file we just uploaded is only visible to us:

We can try to access the file from the terminal (using its URL, displayed under the filename in the properties section of the page), but we will get an **Access denied** error. We can add an extra permission to let everyone read/download the file (assuming, of course, that they know its URL), as the following screenshot illustrates (do not forget to click on **Save** to apply the new access rule):

With this permission in place, the file we uploaded (index.html) is now publicly readable and could be used, for instance, as a static asset for a web application. Just keep in mind that keeping files on S3 is cheap, but it is not free.

Amazon elastic beanstalk

Amazon Elastic Beanstalk (EB) is a simple way of deploying our applications to AWS without having to worry about the various moving parts, such as EC2 and S3, individually. Amazon EB is a sophisticated tool and has great support for Python.

EB is best used from the command line (using the awsebcli package) within a Python virtual environment. The gist of it is that you create a virtual environment for the Python application that you want to deploy to AWS. The application itself is contained in a single directory that serves as a way to package the code to be deployed.

Using the `eb` command-line tool (part of `awsebcli`), one creates an initial deployment configuration (`eb init`), and potentially (that is, usually) customizes this initial configuration by writing additional configuration files (in a directory called `.ebextensions`), specifying options, such as any environment variable needed, or any post installation actions to be performed.

Once the application has been tested locally, it can be deployed to AWS using the `eb create` command, and eventually destroyed using `eb terminate`.

The AWS site has nice tutorials for deploying, for instance, a moderately complex Django web application (`http://docs.aws.amazon.com/elasticbeanstalk/latest/dg/create-deploy-python-django.html#python-django-configure-for-eb`) that could serve as a starting point for you to learn more about EB.

One should note that, despite the fact that most of the EB documentation focuses on web applications, EB is not just for HTTP servers and WSGI apps.

Creating a private cloud

AWS is a great option for a large number of people and companies. At the same time, however, one might realize that the cost of using cloud services from AWS or other providers sometimes adds up to unsustainable levels. Other times, company policies or even data privacy requirements might discourage or even outright forbid the use of cloud resources altogether.

In these cases, one solution could be the creation of an internal, private cloud. This private cloud would use in-house hardware to provide the infrastructure to provision and run virtual machines (a la EC2) as well as a data-storage middleware (similar to what S3 offers), together with other services such as load balancers, database servers, and so on.

There are a number of free, open source, and actively maintained software stacks that make the creation and operation of a private cloud simple (or at least simpler). **OpenStack** (`http://www.openstack.org`), **CloudStack** (`https://cloudstack.apache.org`), and **Eucalyptus** (`http://www.eucalyptus.com`) are three such tools.

What is interesting about the latter one, Eucalyptus, is its ability to interoperate with AWS and in particular with EC2 and S3. The nice consequence of this tight interoperability is the possibility to create an internal cloud that has the same API as AWS. In this way, one could, if necessary or desirable, extend the private cloud with, or even migrate it to, Amazon EC2 and S3 without having to recreate VM images, tools, and administration scripts.

In addition, the boto toolkit that is used to interact with AWS (installable via `pip install boto`) using Python is compatible with Eucalyptus.

Summary

Through AWS, we saw how cloud providers typically offer compute and storage platforms on a pay-as-you-go model, whereby users (that is, us) only pay for the resources that they actually use.

These platforms can be of significant help in both the development phase as well as in operations for our distributed applications. This is especially true for scalability tests, for instance, and in all situations where ordering and provisioning a set of machines ourselves would take too long or represent too expensive an upfront cost. Not to mention the fact that being able to leverage the vast infrastructure and uptime guarantees of a large cloud provider is no small thing.

At the same time, however, one should be aware of the fact that cloud services are not free. They most definitely are not free economically (apart from maybe the first year of use for AWS). Also, they are not free in terms of time and effort, in that they do not free us from knowing how to administer our resources, install the software that we need, and, on top of that, learn the tools and features of whatever provider we choose. Migrating from one cloud provider to another is not always as simple as it should be.

With these caveats in mind, one can start thinking about how and whether a cloud provider could fit into the overall design, development, testing, and deployment cycles of our applications.

A simple strategy, for instance, could be deploying our distributed applications in-house and only using cloud computing to handle surges of demand. To this effect, it might make sense to keep an up-to-date set of VM images at hand and import them into Amazon EC2.

In the next chapter, we will look at a scenario that is very familiar to researchers and folks working in national labs/universities: running Python on a large, high-performance computing (HPC) cluster.

6
Python on an HPC Cluster

In this chapter, we are going to look at yet another way of deploying our distributed Python applications. The method we are going to look at is the use of a **High Performance Computing** (**HPC**) cluster (also called a **supercomputer**), such as the multimillion dollar (or Euros), room-filling machines commonly found in evil overlord lairs.

Real HPC clusters are typically found in universities and national labs and are not what a typical start-up or small company would operate, mostly due to their cost. They are generally quite large systems with possibly hundreds of thousands of CPU cores spread over thousands of machines.

Oftentimes, the maximum size of HPC clusters a center can afford is determined by the amount of electricity that can be delivered to the premises; HPC systems that use a few megawatts are not at all uncommon. The system I work with, for instance, has over 160,000 cores across 7,000 nodes and consumes about 4 megawatts of electricity!

Developers and scientists looking at running Python code on their HPC clusters will find the information in this chapter useful. Those not working on such big systems might find some of the tools mentioned here useful in other settings as well.

Your typical HPC cluster

HPC systems come in all shapes and sizes; however, they tend to share a few common characteristics. They tend to be homogeneous, with a large number of identical, rack-mounted computers located in the same room and connected with very fast networking. Sometimes, especially between upgrades, an HPC cluster might be split into two processor architectures. In those cases, particular care needs to be taken in scheduling our code if those differences have important performance implications.

Most of the computers in a cluster (called **compute nodes**) run exactly the same operating system and the same set of software packages and are dedicated to exclusively run computations, as the name implies. Users are not typically allowed to use these machines directly.

A smaller number of nodes are special in that they are usually not as powerful as the compute nodes but do allow users to log in. They are called **service nodes** (or login nodes or head nodes) and are dedicated to run user scripts, compilations, and utility software for user job management. Users normally log into these nodes to get access to the cluster.

Some other nodes (especially on large installations) are somewhat in-between service nodes and compute nodes; they run the full compute node operating system but are shared by many users, while pure compute nodes tend to run one application thread per core.

These nodes are used for running small serial jobs that do not need the full resources of a compute node (typically, application setups and cleanup phases). On **Cray** systems, for instance, these are called **Multiple Application, Multiple User** (**MAMU**) nodes.

The following public domain photo from NASA shows their 2004 Columbia supercomputer, which at that time had 10,240 processors. Modern installations do not look all that different:

How does one run code on a HPC cluster? Typically, one has to log in to a service node and, from there, interact with a specific piece of software called a **job scheduler**. A job scheduler is a conceptually simple piece of middleware that, given some code to run, will find the most appropriate set of compute nodes to run it.

If no appropriate hardware resources are currently available, the request to run our application will just sit in a queue until enough nodes are free and able to run it. The wait, especially on busy systems, can be quite long and, for small scripts, even longer than the job runtime.

HPC systems use a job scheduler instead of allowing users to log in to compute nodes and freely run their applications there because of the need to ensure fair use of resources across departments and projects as well as the requirement to maximize cluster utilization.

There are a number of job schedulers available both commercially and as open source packages. The most common ones are probably PBS and its derivatives (for example, **Torque** and **PBS Pro**), **HTCondor**, **LoadLeveler**, **SLURM**, **Grid Engine**, and **LSF**. Here, we will briefly introduce two of them: HTCondor and PBS Pro.

Job schedulers

As mentioned in the previous section, you cannot typically run code directly on an HPC cluster but rather must submit a request to run that code to a job scheduler. The job scheduler identifies appropriate compute resources for our application and runs our code on those nodes.

This level of indirection introduces some overhead but also guarantees that every user gets a fair share of the supercomputer time, job priorities are enforced, and that the many cores are kept busy.

The following figure shows the basic components of a job scheduler (for example, PBS or HTCondor) as well as the sequence of events from job submission to execution:

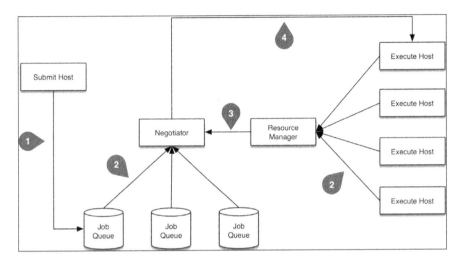

First, let's look at a few definitions:

- **Job**: This is the metadata around our application, such as its executables, any input and output, its hardware and software requirements, its execution environment, and so on
- **Machine**: This is the minimal job execution hardware; it could be a fraction of a physical compute node (for example, one single core of a multicore computer) or a full node, depending on cluster configuration

At a conceptual level, the main parts of a job scheduler are as follows:

- The resource manager
- One or more job queues
- The negotiator

In order to submit a request for work (that is, a job) to the job scheduler, one has to write the metadata object that describes what it is that we want to run and how and where we want to run it. Typically, this involves writing a text file in a specific format, as we will see in the next sections.

Users then submit their job's description files (step 1 in the preceding figure) to the job scheduler using some command-line tools or libraries. These jobs are first put in one or more job queues (for example, there could be a queue for high-priority jobs, one for low-priority jobs, and one for short jobs to use as backfill).

At the same time, the resource manager keeps monitoring (step 2) all compute nodes to keep track of which are free and which are busy. It also keeps track of the priorities of the currently running jobs in case it needs to evict some of them to free some space for high-priority work. In addition, it also keeps track of the requirements of each machine in terms of which jobs it can run (for example, some machines might be reserved to a particular set of users).

Another daemon process, the negotiator, continuously monitors the job queues for idle jobs (step 2) and tries to match them with available machines (step 3), taking into account user priorities, job priorities, job requirements and preferences, and machine requirements and preferences. If no available resources to run a job are identified in this step (called the **negotiation cycle**) and no lower priority, already running job can be evicted, then the job stays in the queue.

Once resources to run the job are identified, the scheduler runs the executable on those machines (step 4). Some schedulers (for example, HTCondor) will optionally copy executable and input files to the execution machines for us. If that is not the case, then we will have to make sure that code and data are either on a shared filesystem or copied over.

The job scheduler (typically using a supervisor daemon) monitors all running jobs, optionally restarting them if they fail. If requested, it is able to send e-mail notifications on job success and/or error.

Most systems support inter-job dependencies so that jobs are executed only after some conditions are met, for instance, the new volume.

Running a Python job using HTCondor

This section assumes access to a cluster managed by the open source HTCondor job scheduler. The installation of HTCondor is not difficult (described in the administrator's manual available at `https://research.cs.wisc.edu/htcondor/manual/`), but it is outside the scope of this book.

HTCondor comes with a set of command-line tools that can be used to submit jobs to the cluster (`condor_submit`), view the status of any submitted job (`condor_q`), kill a job (`condor_rm`), and view the status of all the machines in the cluster (`condor_status`). There are many other tools—more than 60 in total; however, we will concentrate on the four main ones listed in this section.

Another way of interacting with an HTCondor cluster is using the **Distributed Resource Management Application API (DRMAA)**, which comes with most (but not all) HTCondor installations and is packaged as a shared library (for example, `libdrmaa.so` on Linux).

DRMAA abstracts away most of the vendor specificity of major job schedulers so that, in principle, the same code can be used to submit, monitor, and control jobs across clusters and schedulers. The Python `drmaa` module (installable via `pip install drmaa`) provides excellent bindings for DRMAA implementations, including the one provided by HTCondor or PBS.

We are going to concentrate on the command-line tools and see how we can use them to run our code. To do that, we will first create a text file (called **job file** or **submission file**) with the description of what we want to run on the cluster.

Open your favorite text editor and create a new file. The name of this job file does not really matter and there is no standard naming. What we want to do at first is execute the following code on the cluster:

```
$ python3.5 -c "print('Hello, HTCondor!')"
```

For that, our job file (`htcondor/simple/simple.job`) should look like this:

```
# Simple Condor job file
# There is no requirement or standard on job file extensions.
# Format is key = value
# keys and values are case insensitive, with the exception of
# paths and file names (depending on the file system).
# Usage: shell> condor_submit simple.job
# Universe is the execution environment for our jobs
# vanilla is the one for shell scripts etc.
Universe = vanilla
# Executable is the path to the executable to run
Executable = /usr/local/bin/python3.5
# The arguments string is passed to the Executable
# The entire string is enclosed in double-quotes
# Arguments with spaces are in single quotes
# Single & double quotes are escaped by repeating them
Arguments = "-c 'print(''Hello, HTCondor!'')'"
# Output is the file where STDOUT will be redirected to
Output = simple_stdout.txt
# Error is the file where STDERR will be redirected to
Error = simple_stderr.txt
# Log is the HTCondor log, not the log for our app
```

```
Log = simple.log
# Queue tells HTCondor to enqueue our job
Queue
```

The preceding job file is pretty well commented, and so, it should be fairly straightforward (comments start with #).

One common source of confusion is the Output directive, which points to the file for STDOUT redirection and not the output (whatever that might be) of the code that we are executing.

Another source of confusion is the Log directive; it does not point to the log file for our application but rather to the job-specific HTCondor log. The Arguments directive needs some attention as well due to its somewhat peculiar syntax.

We can ask HTCondor to run our simple one-liner using condor_submit as illustrated in the following screenshot, where we submit the job and immediately look at its state with condor_q:

```
(book)bookuser@yippy> condor_submit simple.job; condor_q
Submitting job(s).
1 job(s) submitted to cluster 60.


-- Schedd: yippy
 ID      OWNER            SUBMITTED     RUN_TIME ST PRI SIZE CMD
  60.0   bookuser        1/10 15:24   0+00:00:00 R  0   0.0 python3.5 -c print

1 jobs; 0 completed, 0 removed, 0 idle, 1 running, 0 held, 0 suspended
(book)bookuser@yippy> ls -als
total 64
  0 drwxr-xr-x@ 6 bookuser  staff    204 Jan  8 08:15 .
  0 drwxr-xr-x@ 5 bookuser  staff    170 Jan  9 15:10 ..
  8 -rw-r--r--@ 1 bookuser  staff   1001 Jan  9 11:06 simple.job
 48 -rw-r--r--@ 1 bookuser  staff  23237 Jan 10 15:24 simple.log
  0 -rw-r--r--@ 1 bookuser  staff      0 Jan  7 21:38 simple_stderr.txt
  8 -rw-r--r--@ 1 bookuser  staff     17 Jan 10 15:24 simple_stdout.txt
(book)bookuser@yippy>
```

HTCondor assigns our jobs a numeric identifier of the form cluster id.process id (here, the process ID is specific to HTCondor and not at all the same as the Unix process ID). Since we can submit a potentially large number of jobs in the same job file (one way of achieving this is to pass the number of jobs that we want to start the Queue command, for example, Queue 5000 will start 5,000 instances of our job), HTCondor groups them in what it calls a cluster.

Each cluster has a unique identifier, and each process inside a cluster has an identifier from *0* to *N-1*, where *N* is the total number of processes in the cluster (that is, the number of instances of our job). Since, in our case, we submitted a single job, its identifier is simply **60.0**.

Strictly speaking, job identifiers in the form as described in the preceding section are unique within a single job queue/submit machine and not across the full cluster. What is unique is the so-called `GlobalJobId` the concatenation of the submit hostname, cluster ID, process ID, and the timestamp of when the job was submitted. The value of a job `GlobalJobId`, together with many other internal variables can be displayed using `condor_q -long`.

Depending on the configuration of our HTCondor installation and how busy the cluster is, our job might run immediately or it might sit in the queue for some time. We can check its status with `condor_q` to check whether it is `idle` (status `I`), running (status `R`), suspended (status `H`), or killed (status `X`). Two new states have been added recently: `in the process of transferring data to the execute node` (`>`) and `transferring data back to the submit host` (`<`).

If all goes well, our job will stay idle in the queue for some time, then change its status to running, and finally quit (either successfully or with an error) and disappear from the queue.

Once our job is done, we can look into the current directory and we should see three new files: `simple.log`, `simple_stderr.txt`, and `simple_stdout.txt`. These are the log files for our job, and our job standard error, and standard out streams, respectively.

The log file has many useful pieces of information, including when and from which machine our job was submitted, how long our job had to wait in the job queue, where and when it run, its exit code, and resource utilization.

Hopefully, our simple Python job exited with status zero (meaning success), produced no output on `STDERR` (meaning that `simple_stderr.txt` is empty), and then wrote `Hello, HTCondor!` to `STDOUT` (that is, `simple_stdout.txt`). If not, we will look at how to debug problems later in the chapter.

Let's now submit a simple Python script. The new job file will be quite similar; we just need to change `Executable` and `Arguments` appropriately. We will also pass a couple of environment variables to our job and submit not one but 100 instances, just to make things interesting.

Let's create a new job file (`htcondor/script/script.job`) with the following code:

```
# Simple Condor job file
# There is no requirement or standard on job file extensions.
# Format is key = value
# keys and values are case insensitive, with the exception of
```

```
# paths and file names (depending on the file system).
# Usage: shell> condor_submit script.job


# Universe is the execution environment for our jobs
# vanilla is the one for shell scripts etc.
Universe = vanilla
# Executable is the path to the executable to run
Executable = test.py
# The arguments string is passed to the Executable
# The entire string is enclosed in double-quotes
# Arguments with spaces are in single quotes
# Single & double quotes are escaped by repeating them
Arguments = "--clusterid=$(Cluster) --processid=$(Process)"
# We can specify environment variables for our jobs as
# by default jobs execute in a very restricted environment
Environment = "MYVAR1=foo MYVAR2=bar"
# We can also pass our entire environment to the job
# By default this is not the case (i.e. GetEnv is False)
GetEnv = True
# Output is the file where STDOUT will be redirected to
# We will have one file per process otherwise each
# process will overwrite the same file.
Output = script_stdout.$(Cluster).$(Process).txt
# Error is the file where STDERR will be redirected to
Error = script_stderr.$(Cluster).$(Process).txt
# Log is the HTCondor log, not the log for our app
Log = script.log
# Queue tells HTCondor to enqueue our job
Queue 100
```

Let's then write the Python script that we are going to run. Open a new file (htcondor/script/test.py) using the following code:

```
#!/usr/bin/env python3.5
import argparse
import getpass
import os
```

```
import socket
import sys


ENV_VARS = ('MYVAR1', 'MYVAR2')


parser = argparse.ArgumentParser()
parser.add_argument('--clusterid', type=int)
parser.add_argument('--processid', type=int)
args = parser.parse_args()


cid = args.clusterid
pid = args.processid


print('I am process {} of cluster {}'
      .format(pid, cid))
print('Running on {}'
      .format(socket.gethostname()))
print('$CWD = {}'
      .format(os.getcwd()))
print('$USER = {}'
      .format(getpass.getuser()))


undefined = False
for v in ENV_VARS:
    if v in os.environ:
        print('{} = {}'
              .format(v, os.environ[v]))
    else:
        print('Error: {} undefined'
              .format(v))
        undefined = True
if undefined:
    sys.exit(1)
sys.exit(0)
```

The preceding code is simple but useful when using an HPC cluster for the first time. In fact, it will clearly show where jobs run as well as which user account they run under.

This is all important information to know when writing our Python jobs; some cluster installations have normal user accounts on all compute nodes and share (at least) user home directories across the whole cluster. In these cases, jobs tend to run as the user who submitted them on the login node.

On other installations, jobs are run as an unprivileged user (for example, the user nobody). In these cases, particular thought has to be given to file permissions and the job execution environment.

HTCondor has the ability to efficiently copy data files and/or executables between submit hosts and execution nodes. This can be done on an as-needed basis or a always-copy basis. Interested readers are encouraged to look at the should_transfer_files, transfer_executable, transfer_input_files, and transfer_output_files directives.

There are a couple of interesting things to notice in the preceding job file (htcondor/script/script.job). First, we might need to make sure that the user running our job is able to find Python 3.5 as it might not be in the standard location. We do this by asking HTCondor to pass our entire environment to the running job (that is, via the GetEnv = True directive).

We also submit 100 instances of our script (Queue 100). This is a common pattern for data-parallel applications, where many pieces of data are processed independently of each other by the same code.

We need to customize each instance of our script. We can do this using two variables, $(Process) and $(Cluster), anywhere in the job file to the right of the equals sign. At job submission time, HTCondor replaces them for every process in the job cluster with the corresponding cluster ID and process ID.

We submit this job in the same way as before:

```
$ condor_submit script.job
```

The output of the job submission is shown in the following screenshot (edited to fit in the page):

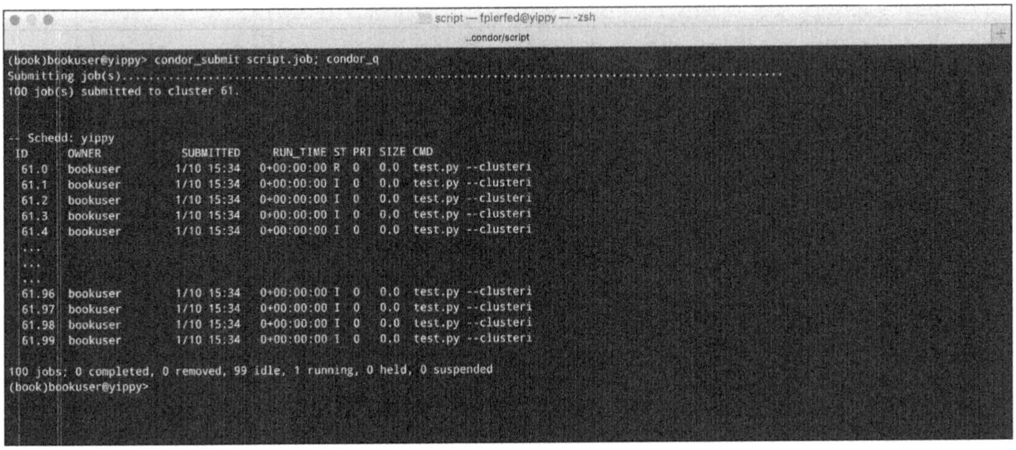

Once all the jobs are done, we will have 100 STDOUT files and 100 STDERR files in the current directory, together with the single log file that HTCondor created for us.

If everything goes well, all the STDERR files will be empty and all of the STDOUT files will have some text along these lines:

```
I am process 9 of cluster 61
Running on somehost
$CWD = /tmp/book/htcondor/script
$USER = bookuser
MYVAR1 = foo
MYVAR2 = bar
```

One interesting exercise, left to you all, is to insert a conditional failure in our test. py script. Something along these lines:

```
if pid == 13:
    raise Exception('Booo!')
else:
    sys.exit(0)
```

Or:

```
if pid == 13:
    sys.exit(2)
else:
    sys.exit(0)
```

Then, see what happens to our job cluster.

If we perform these experiments, we will see that in the first case (an exception being thrown), the corresponding STDERR file will not be empty. The second case, however, is more insidious. The failure will, in fact, be silent, and it will only appear in script.log as an entry of the following form:

```
005 (034.013.000) 01/09 12:25:13 Job terminated.
    (1) Normal termination (return value 2)
        Usr 0 00:00:00, Sys 0 00:00:00  -  Run Remote Usage
        Usr 0 00:00:00, Sys 0 00:00:00  -  Run Local Usage
        Usr 0 00:00:00, Sys 0 00:00:00  -  Total Remote Usage
        Usr 0 00:00:00, Sys 0 00:00:00  -  Total Local Usage
    0  -  Run Bytes Sent By Job
    0  -  Run Bytes Received By Job
    0  -  Total Bytes Sent By Job
    0  -  Total Bytes Received By Job
    Partitionable Resources :    Usage  Request Allocated
        Cpus              :                 1         1
        Disk (KB)         :         1       1  12743407
        Memory (MB)       :         0       1      2048
```

Note that the preceding Normal termination (return value 2) line is the only indication that something went wrong.

Oftentimes, we want to be notified of job failures like these. For this, we can use the following directives in our submission files:

```
Notification = Error
Notify_User = email@example.com
```

This way, in case of an error, HTCondor will send an e-mail to email@example.com with the details of the job that failed. Possible values for notification are Complete (that is, send an e-mail when the job completes, regardless of its exit code), Error (that is, send an e-mail in case of nonzero exit code), and Never, which is the default.

Another quick exercise that is left to you all is to specify which machines our job needs and which ones it prefers. These two independent requests are accomplished via the Requirements and Rank directives, respectively. Requirements is a Boolean expression, while Rank is a floating-point expression. Both are evaluated in every negotiation cycle when HTCondor tries to find a set of machines to run our jobs.

Of all machines for which `Requirements` evaluates to `True`, the ones chosen are those yielding the highest `Rank` object.

> Of course, machines can also define their `Requirements` and `Rank` objects against jobs (this is something done by system administrators). Therefore, a job runs only on machines for which these two `Requirements` expressions are `True`, and for these, the combination of the two `Rank` objects is highest.

If we do not define `Rank` in our job files, it defaults to `0.0`. `Requirements`; defaults to requesting machines with the same architecture and OS as the submit node and enough disk to hold the executable.

We could try some experiments, for instance, we could request machines running on 64-bit Linux with more than 64 GB of RAM and prefer fast machines to slower ones:

```
Requirements = (Target.Memory > 64) && (Target.Arch == "X86_64") &&
(Target.OpSys == "LINUX")

Rank = Target.KFlops
```

> For a list of all possible variables that can be used in `Requirements` and `Rank` expressions, you are encouraged to look at *Machine ClassAd Atributes* in *Appendix A* of the *HTCondor* manual. Probably, the most immediately useful ones are `Target.Memory`, `Target.Arch`, `Target.OpSys`, `Target.Disk`, `Target.Subnet`, and `Target.KFlops`.

Finally, one feature that proves to be extremely powerful in practice is the ability to define dependencies across jobs. Oftentimes, in fact, our application can be decomposed into a number of steps, some of which can be executed concurrently, some of which cannot, maybe because they need to wait for some intermediate result to be ready. In cases where we only have independent steps, we oftentimes just organize them all in a few job clusters as shown in the preceding section.

The HTCondor **DAGMan** (which stands for **Directed Acyclic Graph Manager**) is a meta-scheduler, that is to say a tool that submits jobs, monitors them, and once they are done, it checks which other jobs are ready and submits them.

In order to organize jobs in a DAG, we need to write one submission file per job as usual. In addition, we need to write an extra text file describing the dependency rules among our jobs.

Suppose that we have four jobs (either one-process or multiprocess clusters). Let's call them A, B, C, and D, with submission files a.job, b.job, c.job, and d.job, respectively. Let's say, for example, that we need A to run first. Once A is done, we can run B and C concurrently, and, only after both B and C are done, we can run D.

The following figure illustrates this arrangement graphically:

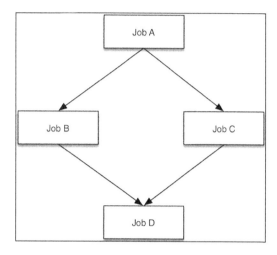

The DAG file (htcondor/dag/simple.dag) that we would have to write in this case is as follows:

```
# Simple Condor DAG file
# There is no requirement or standard on DAG file extensions.
# Usage: shell> condor_submit_dag simple.dag

# Define the nodes in the DAG
JOB A a.job
JOB B b.job
JOB C c.job
JOB D d.job

# Define the relationship between nodes
PARENT A CHILD B C
PARENT B C CHILD D
```

The four submission files do not really matter for this simple example. We could use something along these lines (for example, for job A and similarly for the other three):

```
Universe = vanilla
Executable = /bin/echo
Arguments = "I am job A"
Output = a_stdout.txt
Log = a.log
Queue
```

Submission of the full DAG is achieved using `condor_submit_dag` as follows:

```
$ condor_submit_dag simple.dag
```

The preceding command creates a special submission file (`simple.dag.condor.sub`) for the `condor_dagman` executable, whose job is to monitor our running jobs and schedule the relevant ones at the right time.

The DAGMan meta-scheduler has many features beyond what is shown here, including the Makefile-like ability to resume processing from where it stopped in case of errors.

There are a couple of things that you need to keep in mind about performance. Each node in the DAG, when submitted, has to go through at least one negotiation cycle, just like a regular HTCondor job. These series of cycles introduce an (usually small) overhead that grows proportionally to the number of nodes. Usually, these negotiation cycles overlap with computation, and so we do not see much overhead in practice.

On the other hand, `condor_dagman` is very efficient, to the point that DAGs with a million nodes or more are not uncommon.

 Interested readers are strongly encouraged to read the *DAGMan Applications* chapter of HTCondor.

There is much more about HTCondor that can fit in a short chapter; the full manual is over a 1000 pages long! The information presented here should cover most everyday processing needs. We will cover debugging tips toward the end of the chapter. Next, we will look at another popular job scheduler: PBS.

Running a Python job using PBS

The **Portable Batch System** (**PBS**) was developed for NASA in the beginning of the 90s. It now exists in three variants: OpenPBS, Torque, and PBS Pro. These are all forks of the original codebase, and have a very similar look and feel from the user perspective.

Here, we will look at PBS Pro (which is a commercial product by Altair Engineering and is available at `http://www.pbsworks.com`), but most of the features and directives we will mention should work on Torque and OpenPBS with just some minor differences. Also, in the interest of brevity, we will mostly concentrate on the differences between HTCondor (described earlier) and PBS.

Conceptually, PBS is just like HTCondor, a resource manager and job scheduling system. Both have a similar architecture, with a master node (`pbs_server`), a negotiator and scheduler (`pbs_sched`), and job supervisors (`pbs_mom`) on the execution nodes.

Users submit jobs to a queue. Usually, there are multiple job queues for different types of jobs (for example, serial versus MPI parallel) or jobs of different priorities. HTCondor, in contrast, has one single queue per submit host. Users can interact with PBS either via command-line tools or via DRMAA and its Python `drmaa` bindings (`pip install drmaa`).

PBS job files are normal scripts (for example, Shell or Python scripts) that the user can execute locally. They usually have PBS-specific directives embedded as comments at the top of the script. These directives take the form of `#PBS <directive>` or `REM PBS <directive>` for Windows batch scripts (for example, `#PBS -q serial` or `REM PBS -q serial`).

Jobs are submitted to the appropriate job queue using the `qsub` command, which is the conceptual equivalent of `condor_submit`. Once a job is submitted successfully, `qsub` prints the job ID (in the form `integer.server_hostname`) to the terminal and quits. The job ID is also available to the job itself as the `$PBS_JOBID` environment variable.

Resource requirements and job characteristics are specified either on the `qsub` command line, or using directives in the scripts themselves. It is generally advisable to use directives in the scripts rather than command-line options, as it makes the scripts self-contained and provides a record of how the jobs were submitted.

For example, to submit the exact same `simple.job` job that we discussed in the previous section, you can simply write the following minimal shell script (`pbs/simple/simple.sh`):

```
#!/bin/bash
/usr/local/bin/python3.5 -c "print('Hello, HTCondor!')"
```

As we can see, the preceding script has no PBS directives, which is fine for simple jobs with no requirements. We can submit our script as follows:

```
$ qsub simple.sh
```

Since there should be no reason to write a Shell script for such a simple job, qsub allows us to inline it as follows:

```
$ qsub -- /usr/local/bin/python3.5 -c "print('Hello, HTCondor!')"
```

Not all installations support this feature, however.

On installations with multiple job queues/schedulers, we can specify which queue and/or scheduler to use, either on the command line (that is, `qsub -q queue@scheduler_name`), or in a directive inside the script (that is, `#PBS -q queue@scheduler_name`).

The preceding two example jobs show the difference in philosophy between PBS and HTCondor, at least as far as job submission is concerned. With HTCondor, we need to write a job submission file detailing what it is that we want to run and where we want to run it. With PBS, we can directly submit our scripts or binaries.

> Starting with version 8.0, HTCondor provides a command-line tool, `condor_qsub`, that behaves like a simplified version of `qsub`, and that is mostly useful for transitioning from a PBS installation to a HTCondor pool.

Upon successful submission, qsub prints out our job ID in the form `integer.servername` (for example, `8682293.pbshead`). PBS redirects the job standard streams to `scriptname.oInteger` (for STDOUT) and `scriptname.eInteger` (for STDERR), where `Integer` is the integer part of the job ID (for example, `simple.sh.e8682293` and `script.sh.o8682293` in our example).

Jobs typically run (on the execution hosts) under the same account used for submission, in a temporary directory that PBS creates and removes automatically. The path to this directory is available to the job as the `$PBS_TMPDIR` environment variable.

In general, PBS defines a number of environment variables that are made available to all running jobs. Some are set to the environment of the user account who submitted the job, and their name typically starts with PBS_O (for example, $PBS_O_HOME or $PBS_O_PATH). Others are job specific, such as $PBS_TMPDIR.

 At present, PBS Pro defines 30 variables in the job environment. A full list is available in the *PBS Environment Variables* chapter of the *PBS Professional Reference Guide.*

Job arrays are submitted using the #PBS -J start-end[:step] directive (again, either as an option on the command line or as a directive inside the script). To capture the submitter environment, we would use the -V directive, or we could pass a custom environment to the job using #PBS -v "ENV1=VAL1, ENV2=VAL2, …".

For instance, our job array example from the previous section could be written as follows (pbs/script/test.py):

```
#!/usr/bin/env python3.5
#PBS -J 0-99
#PBS -V
import argparse
import getpass
import os
import socket
import sys


ENV_VARS = ('MYVAR1', 'MYVAR2')

if 'PBS_ENVIRONMENT' in os.environ:
    # raw_cid has the form integer[].server
    raw_cid = os.environ['PBS_ARRAY_ID']
    cid = int(raw_cid.split('[')[0])
    pid = int(os.environ['PBS_ARRAY_INDEX'])
else:
    parser = argparse.ArgumentParser()
    parser.add_argument('--clusterid', type=int)
    parser.add_argument('--processid', type=int)
```

```
    args = parser.parse_args()

    cid = args.clusterid
    pid = args.processid

print('I am process {} of cluster {}'
        .format(pid, cid))
print('Running on {}'
        .format(socket.gethostname()))
print('$CWD = {}'
        .format(os.getcwd()))
print('$USER = {}'
        .format(getpass.getuser()))

undefined = False
for v in ENV_VARS:
    if v in os.environ:
        print('{} = {}'
                .format(v, os.environ[v]))
    else:
        print('Error: {} undefined'
                .format(v))
        undefined = True
if undefined:
    sys.exit(1)
sys.exit(0)
```

We do not need a job submission file at all. We submit the job with qsub as usual, as shown in the following line of code:

```
$ MYVAR1=foo MYVAR2=bar qsub test.py
```

The job ID we get assigned will have the form integer[].server (for example, 8688459[].pbshead) to indicate that we have submitted a job array, not a simple job. This is another difference between HTCondor and PBS; in HTCondor, a simple job is just a job cluster (that is, a job array) with a single process.

Another difference is that the only way a PBS job can access its cluster ID and process ID is via environment variables, as we do not have a job submission file where variables can be substituted at submission time.

With PBS, we also have to do some simple parsing to extract the job array ID from $PBS_ARRAY_ID. However, one nice thing is that we can easily check whether our code is running under PBS by checking whether $PBS_ENVIRONMENT is defined.

Resource requirements are specified using -l directives. For instance, the following directive requests 20 machines, each with 32 cores and 16 GB memory:

```
#PBS -l select=20:ncpus=32:mem=16gb
```

Intra-job dependencies can be specified as well, but not as simply as with HTCondor; the dependency rules need job IDs, which are only known after the jobs have been submitted. The diamond DAG from the previous section could be implemented as follows (pbs/dag/dag.sh):

```
#!/bin/bash
A=`qsub -N A job.sh`
echo "Submitted job A as $A"


B=`qsub -N B -W depend=afterok:$A job.sh`
C=`qsub -N C -W depend=afterok:$A job.sh`
echo "Submitted jobs B & C as $B, $C"


D=`qsub -N D -W depend=afterok:$B:$C job.sh`
echo "Submitted job D as $D"
```

Here, the job script itself is as simple as the following:

```
#!/bin/bash
echo "I am job $PBS_JOBNAME"
```

In the preceding example, it is interesting to note the use of $PBS_JOBNAME to get the user-supplied job name and the use of -W depend= directives to enforce job execution sequencing.

Once jobs are submitted, we can monitor them using the qstat command, which is the equivalent of condor_q. Killing a job (or removing it from the queue before it runs) is done via qdel (the equivalent of condor_rm).

PBS Pro, just like HTCondor, is a complex system with a large number of features. What we discussed so far has just scratched the surface of what PBS can do, but it should serve as a starting point for those of you who want to run code on a PBS HPC cluster.

Some find the ability to submit Python or Shell scripts directly to PBS without the need for a job file very attractive. Others sorely miss tools such as HTCondor DAGMan to handle intra-job dependencies. In the end, however, PBS and HTCondor are very capable systems in use on some of the largest HPC clusters today.

Debugging

Everything is great when things work as we expect them to; oftentimes, however, we are not so lucky. Distributed applications, and even simple jobs running remotely, are particularly challenging to debug. It is usually hard to know exactly which user account our jobs run under, which environment they are executed in, where they run, and, with job schedulers, it is even hard to predict when they will run.

When things do not work as we expect them to, there are a few places where we could get some hints as to what happened. When working with a job scheduler, the first thing to do is look at any error messages returned by the job submission tool (that is, `condor_submit`, `condor_submit_dag`, or `qsub`). The second place to look for clues are the job `STDOUT`, `STDERR`, and log files.

Usually, the job scheduler itself has tools to diagnose problematic jobs. HTCondor, for instance, provides `condor_q -better-analyze` to investigate why a given job might be stuck in the queue longer than expected.

In general, common sources of problems for applications managed by a job scheduler fall into these broad categories:

- Insufficient privileges
- Incorrect environments
- Restricted network communications
- Code dependency problems
- Job requirements
- Shared versus local filesystem

While the first three are usually fairly simple to diagnose by submitting a test job that simply prints out the full environment, the username, and so on, the others can be very tricky to trace down, especially on large clusters.

In those cases, it is often useful to note on which machines our job was running and then start an interactive session (that is, `qsub -I` or `condor_submit - interactive` or even `condor_ssh_to_job`) and replay the code step by step.

If our jobs request either resources that are not abundant (for example, a very specific version of the OS or software packages or some specialized hardware) or too many resources, then the job scheduler will have a hard time finding a time when those are available.

Job schedulers typically offer tools to check which resources satisfy our job requirements now (for example, `condor_status -constrain`). If our jobs do not seem to be assigned to compute nodes fast enough (or ever), it is worth performing a sanity check on our job requirements.

Another source of potential problem stems from using code and/or data on filesystems that are available on the submit host but not on all of compute nodes. In these cases, the use of data transfer facilities (like the one provided by HTCondor) or data-staging preprocessing scripts is highly recommended.

A common approach for Python code is to have a setup job that creates a Python virtual environment and installs all the dependencies (specifying exact versions) first. Once this is done, the real application is submitted to the job scheduler.

In some applications, the amount of data to be moved is so large that the data transfer would take up a significant fraction of the processing time. In these cases, it is usually best to move the processing to the data, even if it means using fewer or slower machines. If that is not possible, one should try to schedule data movements just like a regular job and use inter-job dependencies to make sure that the computation starts only after the relevant data has been staged.

Summary

We saw how we can run our Python code on an HPC cluster using a job scheduler such as HTCondor or PBS.

Many aspects were not covered in the chapter due to space constraints. Probably, the most notable is **MPI** (**Message Passing Interface**), which is the main interprocess communication library standard for HPC jobs. Python has bindings for MPI, and probably the most commonly used one is **mpi4py**, which is available at `http://pythonhosted.org/mpi4py/` and on the Python Package Index (`https://pypi.python.org/pypi/mpi4py/`).

Another topic that did not fit in the chapter is the ability to run distributed task queues on an HPC cluster. For those types of applications, one could submit a series of jobs to the cluster; one job would start the message broker, some other jobs could start the workers, and finally, one last job could start the application itself. Particular care should be paid to connecting workers and applications to the broker that will be running on a machine not known at submission time. A strategy similar to the one used by Pyro (discussed in *Chapter 4, Distributed Applications – with Celery*), namely, the use of a name server would be one way to address the problem.

However, having persistent processes on compute nodes on an HPC cluster is rarely viewed with benevolence by system administrators as it defeats the purpose of having a job scheduler. Most installations will terminate long-running processes after a number of hours. For this type of application, it is always better to consult the administrators first.

Job schedulers (and MPI as well) are truly effective tools that have a place outside the HPC world. Many are open source with a very active community and are very much worth a look.

The next chapter will talk about the very important topic of what to do when things go wrong in a distributed application.

7

Testing and Debugging Distributed Applications

Distributed systems, both large and small, can be extremely challenging to test and debug, as they are spread over a network, run on computers that can be quite different from each other, and might even be physically located in different continents altogether.

Moreover, the computers we use could have different user accounts, different disks with different software packages, different hardware resources, and very uneven performance. Some can even be in a different time zone. Developers of distributed systems need to consider all these pieces of information when trying to foresee failure conditions. Operators have to work around all of these challenges when debugging errors.

So far, in this book, we have not spent much time on the extremely important issue of what to do when something goes either wrong or differently than we expect, and we instead concentrated on some of the tools that we can use to write and deploy our applications.

In this chapter, we will look at some of the problems that developers of distributed systems are likely to encounter. We will also explore some solutions to these challenges and some tools that can come to the rescue.

The big picture

Testing and debugging monolithic applications is not simple, as every developer knows. However, there are a number of tools that make the task dramatically easier, including the **pdb** debugger, various profilers (notable mentions include **cProfile** and **line_profile**), linters, static code analysis tools, and a host of test frameworks, a number of which have been included in the standard library of Python 3.3 and higher.

The challenge with distributed applications is that most of the tools and packages that we can use for single-process applications lose much of their power when dealing with multiple processes, especially when these processes run on different computers.

Debugging and profiling distributed applications written in C, C++, and Fortran can be done with tools such as **Intel VTune**, **Allinea MAP**, and **DDT**. Unfortunately, Python developers are left with very few or no options for the time being.

Writing small- or medium-sized distributed systems is not terribly hard, as we saw in the pages so far. The main difference between writing monolithic programs and distributed applications is that the latter are made up of many inter-dependent components which often run on different hardware and which have to coordinate their work. This is what makes monitoring and debugging distributed code harder and less convenient.

Fortunately, we can still use all familiar debuggers and code analysis tools on our Python distributed applications. Unfortunately, these tools will only go so far to the point that we will have to rely on old-fashioned logging and print statements to get the full picture on what went wrong.

Common problems – clocks and time

Time is a handy variable for use. For instance, using timestamps is very natural when we want to join different streams of data, sort database records, and in general, reconstruct the timeline for a series of events, which we oftentimes observe out of order. In addition, some tools (for example, GNU make) rely solely on file modification time and are easily confused by a clock skew between machines.

For these reasons, clock synchronization among all computers and systems we use is very important. If our computers are in different time zones, we might want to not only synchronize their clocks but also set them to **Coordinated Universal Time** (**UTC**) for simplicity. In all the cases, when changing clocks to UTC is not possible, a good piece of advice is to always process time in UTC within our code and to only convert to local time for display purposes.

In general, clock synchronization in distributed systems is a fascinating and complex topic, and it is out of the scope of this book. Most readers, luckily, are likely to be well served by the **Network Time Protocol** (**NTP**), which is a perfectly fine synchronization solution for most situations. Most modern operating systems, including Windows, Mac OS X, and Linux, have great support for NTP.

Another thing to consider when talking about time is the timing of periodic actions, such as polling loops or cronjobs. Many applications need to spawn processes or perform actions (for example, sending a confirmation e-mail or checking whether new data is available) at regular intervals.

A common pattern is to set up timers (either in our code or via the tools provided by the OS) and have all these timers go off at some time, usually at a specific hour and at regular intervals after that. The risk of this approach is that we can overload the system the very moment all these processes wake up and start their work.

A surprisingly common example would be starting a significant number of processes that all need to read some configuration or data file from a shared disk. In these cases, everything goes fine until the number of processes becomes so large that the shared disk cannot handle the data transfer, thus slowing our application to a crawl.

A common solution is the staggering of these timers in order to spread them out over a longer time interval. In general, since we do not always control all code that we use, it is good practice to start our timers at some random number of minutes past the hour, just to be safe.

Another example of this situation would be an image-processing service that periodically polls a set of directories looking for new data. When new images are found, they are copied to a staging area, renamed, scaled, and potentially converted to a common format before being archived for later use. If we're not careful, it would be easy to overload the system if many images were to be uploaded at once.

A better approach would be to throttle our application (maybe using a queue-based architecture) so that it would only start an appropriately small number of image processors so as to not flood the system.

Common problems – software environments

Another common challenge is making sure that the software installed on all the various machines we are ever going to use is consistent and consistently upgraded.

Unfortunately, it is frustratingly common to spend hours debugging a distributed application only to discover that for some unknown and seemingly impossible reason, some computers had an old version of the code and/or its dependencies. Sometimes, we might even find the code to have disappeared completely.

The reasons for these discrepancies can be many: from a mount point that failed, to a bug in our deployment procedures, to a simple human mistake.

A common approach, especially in the HPC world, is to always create a self-contained environment for our code before launching the application itself. Some projects go as far as preferring static linking of all dependencies to avoid having the runtime pick up the wrong version of a dynamic library.

This approach works well if the application runtime is long compared to the time it takes to build its full environment, all of its software dependencies, and the application itself. It is not that practical otherwise.

Python, fortunately, has the ability to create self-contained virtual environments. There are two related tools that we can use: `pyvenv` (available as part of the Python 3.5 standard library) and `virtualenv` (available in **PyPI**). Additionally, `pip`, the Python package management system, allows us to specify the exact version of each package we want to install in a requirements file. These tools, when used together, permit reasonable control on the execution environment.

However, the devil, as it is often said, is in the details, and different computer nodes might use the exact same Python virtual environment but incompatible versions of some external library.

In this respect, container technologies such as **Docker** (`https://www.docker.com`) and, in general, version-controlled virtual machines are promising ways out of the software runtime environment maelstrom.

In cases where container technologies cannot be used, HPC clusters come to mind, the best approach will probably be to not rely on the system software and manage our own environments and the full-software stack.

Common problems – permissions and environments

Different computers might run our code under different user accounts, and our application might expect to be able to read a file or write data into a specific directory and hit an unexpected permission error. Even in cases where the user accounts used by our code are all the same (down to the same user ID and group ID), their environment may be different on different hosts. Therefore, an environment variable we assumed to be defined might not be or, even worse, might be set to an incompatible value.

These problems are common when our code runs as a special, unprivileged user, such as `nobody`. Defensive coding, especially when accessing the environment, and making sure to always fall back to sensible defaults when variables are undefined (that is, `value = os.environ.get('SOME_VAR', fallback_value)` instead of simply `value = os.environ.get['SOME_VAR']`) is often necessary.

A common approach, when this is possible, is to only run our applications under a specific user account that we control and specify the full set of environment variables our code needs in the deployment and application startup scripts (which will have to be version controlled as well).

Some systems, however, not only execute jobs under extremely limited user accounts, but they also restrict code execution to temporary sandboxes. In many cases, access to the outside network is also blocked. In these situations, one might have no other choice but to set up the full environment locally and copy it to a shared disk partition. Other data can be served from custom-build servers running as ancillary jobs just for this purpose.

In general, permission problems and user environment mismatches are very similar to problems with the software environment and should be tackled in concert. Often times, developers find themselves wanting to isolate their code from the system as much as possible and create a small, but self-contained environment with all the code and all the environment variables they need.

Common problems – the availability of hardware resources

The hardware resources that our application needs might or might not be available at any given point in time. Moreover, even if some resources were to be available at some point in time, nothing guarantees that they will stay available for much longer. A problem we can face related to this is network glitches, which are quite common in many environments (especially for mobile apps) and which, for most practical purposes, are indistinguishable from machine or application crashes.

Applications using a distributed computing framework or job scheduler can often rely on the framework itself to handle at least some common failure scenarios. Some job schedulers will even resubmit our jobs in case of errors or sudden machine unavailability.

Complex applications, however, might need to implement their own strategies to deal with hardware failures. In some cases, the best strategy is to simply restart the application when the necessary resources are available again.

Other times, restarting from scratch would be cost prohibitive. In these cases, a common approach is to implement application checkpointing. What this means is that the application both writes its state to a disk periodically and is able to bootstrap itself from a previously saved state.

In implementing a checkpointing strategy, you need to balance the convenience of being able to restart an application midway with the performance hit of writing its state to a disk. Another consideration is the increase in code complexity, especially when many processes or threads are involved in reading and writing state information.

A good rule of thumb is that data or results that can be recreated easily and quickly do not warrant implementation of application checkpointing. If, on the other hand, some processing requires a significant amount of time and one cannot afford to waste it, then application checkpointing might be in order.

For example, climate simulations can easily run for several weeks or months at a time. In these cases, it is important to checkpoint them every hour or so, as restarting from the beginning after a crash would be expensive. On the other hand, a process that takes an uploaded image and creates a thumbnail for, say, a web gallery, runs quickly and is not normally worth checkpointing.

To be safe, state should always be written and updated atomically (for example, by writing to a temporary file and replacing the original only after the write completes successfully). The last thing we want is to restart from a corrupted state!

Very familiar to HPC users as well as users of AWS spot instances is a situation where a fraction or the entirety of the processes of our application are evicted from the machines that they are running on. When this happens, a warning is typically sent to our processes (usually, a SIGQUIT signal) and after a few seconds, they are unceremoniously killed (via a SIGKILL signal). For AWS spot instances, the time of termination is available through a web service in the instance metadata. In either case, our applications are given some time to save the state and quit in an orderly fashion.

Python has powerful facilities to catch and handle signals (refer to the signal module). For example, the following simple code show how we can implement a bare-bones checkpointing strategy in our application:

```python
#!/usr/bin/env python3.5
"""
Simple example showing how to catch signals in Python
"""
import json
import os
import signal
import sys



# Path to the file we use to store state. Note that we assume
# $HOME to be defined, which is far from being an obvious
# assumption!
STATE_FILE = os.path.join(os.environ['HOME'],
                                '.checkpoint.json')



class Checkpointer:
    def __init__(self, state_path=STATE_FILE):
        """
        Read the state file, if present, and initialize from that.
        """
        self.state = {}
        self.state_path = state_path
        if os.path.exists(self.state_path):
            with open(self.state_path) as f:
                self.state.update(json.load(f))
```

```
        return

    def save(self):
        print('Saving state: {}'.format(self.state))
        with open(self.state_path, 'w') as f:
            json.dump(self.state, f)
        return

    def eviction_handler(self, signum, frame):
        """
        This is the function that gets called when a signal is trapped.
        """
        self.save()

        # Of course, using sys.exit is a bit brutal. We can do better.
        print('Quitting')
        sys.exit(0)
        return


if __name__ == '__main__':
    import time

    print('This is process {}'.format(os.getpid()))

    ckp = Checkpointer()
    print('Initial state: {}'.format(ckp.state))

    # Catch SIGQUIT
    signal.signal(signal.SIGQUIT, ckp.eviction_handler)

    # Get a value from the state.
    i = ckp.state.get('i', 0)
    try:
        while True:
            i += 1
            ckp.state['i'] = i
```

```
    print('Updated in-memory state: {}'.format(ckp.state))
    time.sleep(1)
except KeyboardInterrupt:
    ckp.save()
```

We can run the preceding script in a terminal window and then in another terminal window, we send it a SIGQUIT signal (for example, via kill -s SIGQUIT <process id>). If we do this, we see the checkpointing in action, as the following screenshot illustrates:

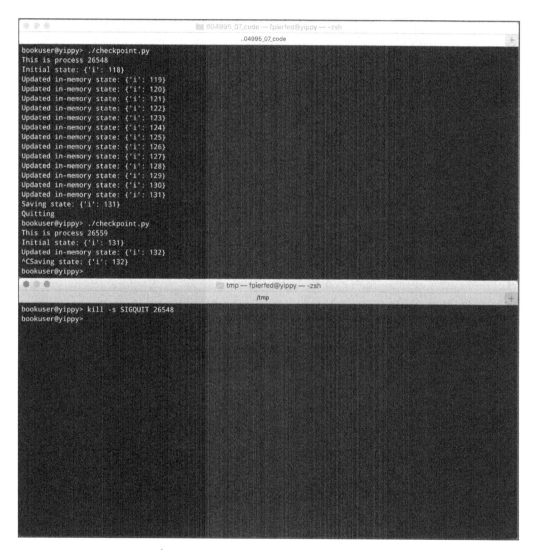

A common situation in distributed applications is that of being forced to run code in potentially heterogeneous environments: machines (real or virtual) of different performances, with different hardware resources (for example, with or without GPUs), and potentially different software environments (as we mentioned already).

Even in the presence of a job scheduler, to help us choose the right software and hardware environment, we should always log the full environment as well as the performance of each execution machine. In advanced architectures, these performance metrics can be used to improve the efficiency of job scheduling.

PBS Pro, for instance, takes into consideration the historical performance figures of each job being submitted to decide where to execute it next. **HTCondor** continuously benchmarks each machine and makes those figures available for node selection and ranking.

Perhaps the most frustrating cases are where, either due to the network itself or due to servers being overloaded, network requests take so long that our code hits its internal timeouts. This might lead us to believe that the counterpart service is not available. These bugs, especially when transient, can be quite hard to debug.

Challenges – the development environment

Another common challenge in distributed systems is the setup of a representative development and testing environment, especially for individuals or small teams. Ideally, in fact, the development environment should be identical to the worst-case scenario deployment environment. It should allow developers to test common failure scenarios, such as a disk filling up, varying network latencies, intermittent network connections, hardware and software failures, and so on—all things that are bound to happen in real time, sooner or later.

Large teams have the resources to set up development and test clusters, and they almost always have dedicated software quality teams stress testing our code.

Small teams, unfortunately, often find themselves forced to write code on their laptops and use a very simplified (and best-case scenario!) environment made up of two or three virtual machines running on the laptops themselves to emulate the real system.

This pragmatic solution works and is definitely better than nothing. However, we should remember that virtual machines running on the same host exhibit unrealistically high-availability and low-network latencies. In addition, nobody will accidentally upgrade them without us knowing or upgrade them with the wrong operating system. The environment is simply too controlled and stable to be realistic.

A step closer to a realistic setup would be to create a small development cluster on, say, AWS, using the same VM images, with the same software stack and user accounts that we are going to use in production.

All that said, there is simply no replacement for the real thing. For cloud-based applications, it is worth our while to *at least* test our code on a smaller version of the deployment setup. For HPC applications, we should be using either a test cluster, a partition of the operational cluster, or a test queue for development and testing.

Ideally, we would develop on an exact clone of the operational system. Cost consideration and ease of development will constantly push us to the multiple-VMs-on-a-laptop solution; it is simple, essentially free, and it works without an Internet connection, which is an important point.

We should, however, keep in mind that distributed applications are not impossibly hard to write; they just have more failure modes than their monolithic counterparts do. Some of these failure modes (especially those related to data access patterns) typically require a careful choice of architecture.

Correcting architectural choices dictated by false assumptions later on in the development stage can be costly. Convincing managers to give us the hardware resources that we need early on is usually difficult. In the end, this is a delicate balancing act.

A useful strategy – logging everything

Oftentimes, logging is like taking backups or eating vegetables—we all know we should do it, but most of us forget. In distributed applications, we simply have no other choice—logging is essential. Not only that, logging everything is essential.

With many different processes running on potentially ephemeral remote resources at difficult-to-predict times, the only way to understand what happens is to have logging information and have it readily available and in an easily searchable format/system.

At the bare minimum, we should log process startup and exit time, exit code and exceptions (if any), all input arguments, all outputs, the full execution environment, the name and IP of the execution host, the current working directory, the user account as well as the full application configuration, and all software versions.

The idea is that if something goes wrong, we should be able to use this information to log onto the same machine (if still available), go to the same directory, and reproduce exactly what our code was doing. Of course, being able to exactly reproduce the execution environment might simply not be possible (oftentimes, because it requires administrator privileges).

However, we should always aim to be able to recreate a good approximation of that environment. This is where job schedulers really shine; they allow us to choose a specific machine and specify the full job environment, which makes replicating failures easier.

Logging software versions (not only the version of the Python interpreter, but also the version of all the packages used) helps diagnose outdated software stacks on remote machines. The Python package manager, `pip`, makes getting the list of installed packages easy: `import pip; pip.main(['list'])`. Whereas, `import sys; print(sys.executable, sys.version_info)` displays the location and version of the interpreter.

It is also useful to create a system whereby all our classes and function calls emit logging messages with the same level of detail and at the same points in the object life cycle. Common approaches involve the use of decorators and, maybe a bit too esoteric for some, metaclasses. This is exactly what the `autologging` Python module (available on PyPI) does for us.

Once logging is in place, we face the question of where to store all these logging messages whose traffic could be substantial for high verbosity levels in large applications. Simple installations will probably want to write log messages to text files on a disk. More complex applications might want to store these messages in a database (which can be done by creating a custom handler for the Python logging module) or in specialized log aggregators such as **Sentry** (`https://getsentry.com`).

Closely related to logging is the issue of monitoring. Distributed applications can have many moving parts, and it is often essential to know which machines are up and which are busy, as well as which processes or jobs are currently running, waiting, or in an error state. Knowing which processes are taking longer than usual to complete their work is often an important warning sign that something might be wrong.

Several monitoring solutions for Python (oftentimes, integrated with our logging system) exist. The Celery project, for instance, recommends `flower` (`http://flower.readthedocs.org`) as a monitoring and control web application. HPC job schedulers, on the other hand, tend to lack common, general-purpose monitoring solutions that go beyond simple command-line clients.

Monitoring comes in handy in discovering potential problems before they become serious. It is in fact useful to monitor resources, such as available disk space and trigger actions, or even simple warning e-mails, when they fall under a given threshold. Many centers monitor hardware performance and hard drive SMART data to detect early signs of potential problems.

These issues are more likely to be of interest to operations personnel rather than developers, but they are useful to keep in mind. They can also be integrated in our applications to implement appropriate strategies in order to handle performance degradations gracefully.

A useful strategy – simulating components

A good, although possibly expensive in terms of time and effort, test strategy is to simulate some or all of the components of our system. The reasons are multiple; on one hand, simulating or mocking software components allows us to test our interfaces to them more directly. In this respect, mock testing libraries, such as `unittest.mock` (part of the Python 3.5 standard library), are truly useful.

Another reason to simulate software components is to make them fail or misbehave on demand and see how our application responds. For instance, we could increase the response time of services such as REST APIs or databases, to worst-case scenario levels and see what happens. Sometimes, we might exceed timeout values in some network calls leading our application to incorrectly assume that the server has crashed.

Especially early on in the design and development of a complex distributed application, one can make overly optimistic assumptions about things such as network availability and performance or response time of services such as databases or web servers. For this reason, having the ability to either completely bring a service offline or, more subtly, modify its behavior, can tell us a lot about which of the assumptions in our code might be overly optimistic.

The **Netflix Chaos Monkey** (`https://github.com/Netflix/SimianArmy`) approach of disabling random components of our system to see how our application copes with failures can be quite useful.

Summary

Writing and running small- or medium-sized distributed applications in Python is not hard. There are many high-quality frameworks that we can leverage among others, for example, Celery, Pyro, various job schedulers, Twisted, MPI bindings (not discussed in this book), or the `multiprocessing` module in the standard library.

The real difficulty, however, lies in monitoring and debugging our applications, especially because a large fraction of our code runs concurrently on many different, often remote, computers.

The most insidious bugs are those that end up producing incorrect results (for example, because of data becoming corrupted along the way) rather than raising an exception, which most frameworks are able to catch and bubble up.

The monitoring and debugging tools that we can use with Python code are, sadly, not as sophisticated as the frameworks and libraries we use to develop that same code. The consequence is that large teams end up developing their own, oftentimes, very specialized, distributed debugging systems from scratch and small teams mostly rely on log messages and print statements.

More work is needed in the area of debuggers for distributed applications in general and for dynamic languages such as Python in particular.

8
The Road Ahead

This has been a quick, and hopefully interesting journey into the world of parallel and distributed computing with Python. What this book has really tried to do is convince you that writing a small- to medium-sized distributed applications with Python is not only within the reach of most developers, but it is also quite simple.

Sure, there are a lot of moving parts in even a simple distributed application—possibly, many more than in a regular monolithic application. There are, more critically, also a lot more failure scenarios and a lot many things happening at the same time on different machines.

Luckily, however, there are several high-quality, well-tested Python libraries and frameworks that you can easily leverage to write distributed systems in a much easier way than most of us might think.

Furthermore, parallel and distributed computing is rapidly becoming mainstream, and with the introduction of *many-core* CPUs (that is, CPUs with a relatively high number of cores, each of which are quite weak computationally) in the very near future, writing parallel code might very well be a necessity if we are to keep abreast of **Moore's law** for the years to come.

Tools such as Celery, Python-RQ, or Pyro, among others, allow all Python developers to reap significant benefits in terms of raw performance with relatively little effort.

One sore point, which must be recognized, is the lack of powerful debuggers and profilers for distributed applications, which is a serious problem that is not unique to Python. Monitoring solutions and log aggregators do exist and help in identifying performance bottlenecks and tracking down bugs. The situation, however, should be improved.

The rest of this chapter looks back at the ground that we have covered so far and tries to put what you have learned in perspective. It also offers advanced readers some suggestions as to which tools and topics to pursue further.

The first two chapters

The initial chapters of this book provided you with some of the basic theories of parallel and distributed computing. They introduced a number of important concepts such as shared memory and distributed memory architectures and their differences.

They also looked at the basic arithmetic of code speedup by parallelization in terms of **Amdahl's law**. The main lesson of that discussion was that after a while, the efforts put into parallelizing an existing algorithm start to outweigh the performance gains. Also as mentioned, one way to *side step* Amdahl's law is to increase the problem size and have the parallel parts of our code do more work with respect to the serial parts (**Gustafson's law**).

The other lesson from Amdahl's law is to try and keep interprocess communication within our applications as small as possible. Ideally, our processes should be completely independent from each other. Little or no interprocess crosstalk reduces code complexity as well as general overhead.

Most real-world scenarios require a series of fan-out and fan-in synchronization/reduction steps, which most frameworks handle reasonably efficiently. Data dependencies or heavy messaging in parallel steps, however, usually become a huge headache.

Another architecture that we briefly mentioned is that of *data trains* or data parallelism. This is that form of processing where one typically launches significantly more worker processes than the number of available hardware resources. As we saw, the main advantages of data parallelism are nice scaling properties and simpler code. In addition, most operating systems and job schedulers will do a decent job at interleaving I/O and computation, thus hiding system latency.

We have also looked at two quite different programming paradigms: synchronous and asynchronous programming. We saw how Python has excellent support for futures, callbacks, and coroutines, which are central to asynchronous programming.

Asynchronous code has, as we discussed, the nice advantage of side stepping or at least lessening, race conditions, since only one piece of code can run at any given point in time. This means that data access patterns are greatly simplified at the cost of some code and debugging complexity; it is generally difficult to follow the execution path when coroutines and callbacks are involved.

Throughout the book, we looked at concurrent code performances using threads, multiple processes, and coroutines. In the case of I/O operations, we saw how all three concurrency strategies can achieve significant speedups. Due to the Python GIL, however, CPU operations do not scale well or at all, as we saw, unless multiple processes are used.

Both synchronous and asynchronous programming have their merits. As far as concurrency goes, threads will definitely look familiar to developers coming from system programming in C and C++. Coroutines have a really big advantage of avoiding, for the most part, race conditions. Multiple processes, while possibly quite heavyweight on a single machine, pave the way for more general distributed computing architectures. Which style to use depends on personal preferences and on the specific libraries one has to use.

The tools

In *Chapter 3, Parallelism in Python*, we looked at a few standard library modules that can be used to introduce (single-node) parallelism in our applications. We experimented with both the `threading` and `multiprocessing` modules directly and via the higher-level `concurrent.futures` module.

We saw how, for non-distributed, parallel applications, Python offers a really robust foundation. The preceding three modules are complete and included in every modern Python distribution. They have no external dependencies, which makes them quite appealing.

We explored a few third-party Python modules for simple distributed computing in *Chapter 4, Distributed Applications – with Celery*. These included Celery, Python-RQ, and Pyro. We saw how to use them in our code, and mostly, we saw how simple it is to get up and running with each one of them.

They all require some pieces of infrastructure such as message brokers, databases, or name servers, and so they might or might not be of use in all contexts. At the same time, they all allow developers to write small- to medium-sized distributed applications fairly easily. They are, most importantly, reasonably well supported by an active community.

The general wisdom regarding performance-critical code in Python is that one should always profile each application to find out which parts of the code need optimizing. If the use of a faster interpreter such as `pypy`, does not make enough of a difference, one should investigate the use of optimized libraries such as `numpy` for numerical code and the use of C or **Cython** extensions that can provide quite a performance boost.

If these steps are not sufficient or practical, then one should start looking at concurrency, parallelism, and distributed computing, since these introduce important complexities.

One simple option is to opt for data parallelism wherever possible (for example, launching many instances of code against different pieces of data). This is where a job scheduler such as HTCondor can be extremely useful.

More complex, but still reasonably easy options are the use of modules such as `concurrent.futures` or Celery to achieve code parallelism. Advanced users, especially on HPC clusters, might want to investigate the use of MPI as an interprocess communication framework.

Not all distributed applications, however, lend themselves to being efficiently implemented using Celery, Python-RQ, or Pyro. This is especially true for applications requiring complex, high-performance, distributed processing graphs, which is an area where tools such as Celery are not particularly strong.

In these cases, developers could investigate the applicability of workflow management systems, such as **Luigi** (`https://github.com/spotify/luigi`), or even stream processing such as Apache Spark or Storm. For Python-specific tools, refer to `https://spark.apache.org/docs/0.9.1/python-programming-guide.html` and `https://github.com/Parsely/streamparse`.

The cloud and the HPC world

Chapter 5, Python in the Cloud, gave you a quick tour of the cloud in general and Amazon Web Services in particular. This is a hot topic nowadays, and the reason for this is simple: with relatively little upfront investment and virtually no wait, one can rent a few virtual machines together with, optionally, a database server and a data store. If the application needs more power, one can simply scale up the underlying infrastructure with the press of a button (and the swipe of a credit card).

Things, unfortunately, are never as simple as vendor brochures like to depict, especially when outsourcing a critical piece of infrastructure to a third party whose interests might not be perfectly aligned with ours.

A solid piece of advice is to always plan for the worst and keep automatic backups of the whole application and its software stack locally (or at the very least, on a separate provider). Ideally (but not that practically), one would have a scaled-down, but up-to-date copy of the full application on a completely separate cloud provider as a form of insurance against provider outages and vendor lock ins.

Having local backups is extremely important when relying on infrastructure-as-a-service providers. News of customer VMs and data being deleted or not being reachable, either as a policy or mistake are not uncommon. Vendor lock in is another serious concern, especially when an application grows to the point of being quite expensive to adapt to another provider and their specific APIs and services.

Restricting oneself to the lowest common denominator (for example, just using EC2 from AWS) can be both tempting and frustrating, as one would have to reimplement all the advanced services that, say, AWS provides already.

All in all, the cloud is a bit of a double-edged sword. It is certainly convenient and cost effective for small teams and small applications. It can be quite expensive for large applications or applications processing large amounts of data as the bandwidth tends to be quite costly.

In addition, teams in academic, governmental, or inter-governmental institutions might find it difficult to acquire the funds necessary to pay for a cloud provider. In these centers, in fact, it is usually easier to get funding to buy infrastructure rather than services.

Another concern about cloud computing which severely limits its applicability in many instances, is the issue of data privacy and data hosting. Large corporations, for instance, tend to be reluctant to host their own private, and often confidential, data on machines that they do not own.

Medical data or, in general, data that can be uniquely associated to customers or patients has its own set of legal restrictions on where and how it should be hosted. Recent revelations about state-sponsored surveillance in the U.S. are making European companies take a hard look at the privacy and legal jurisdiction of their data when hosted on the cloud.

High-performance computing, which was discussed in *Chapter 6, Python on a HPC Cluster*, has been around for several decades, yet the tools its community developed over all these years are still largely relegated to the HPC world and have not made serious inroads in the more general, distributed computing landscape.

While there are surely several reasons for this, one should definitely explore at least open source job schedulers, such as HTCondor, and their applicability to the problem at hand. HTCondor is actively developed and is used in many different contexts. It could be a formidable, distributed computing middleware for small and large applications.

Modern job schedulers offer a large set of features that are especially strong in the fields of fault tolerance, workflow management, and the scheduling of data movements. They all support running arbitrary executables, which means that they can all schedule and run Python code with no difficulty.

Interesting to some will be the ability to dynamically extend an HPC system with virtual machines provisioned on the cloud. Some job schedulers have native support for this using adapters such as **Eucalyptus**.

Advanced HPC users might want to customize their applications to a particular HPC cluster morphology in use at their institution. Oftentimes, in fact, the network fabric in an HPC system is organized in a hierarchy: very fast interconnects link nodes on the same blades. The next performance tier connects blades in the same cabinet or a set of cabinets. The Infiniband-grade fabric connects the rest of the cabinet groups and, finally, slower Ethernet links clusters, with each other and to the outside world.

The consequence is that applications that require heavy interprocess communication and/or large data movements can oftentimes achieve significantly higher performance using a smaller number of processors located on the same blade rather than a larger number of CPUs across blades and potentially racks. Similar considerations apply to the specifics of the network filesystem used and whether or not one pays a penalty for heavy file metadata operations.

The downside of these optimizations, of course, is that they are not fully portable, which is compounded by the fact that HPC systems have a typical life span of only a few years, thus requiring a constant upkeep of the code for maximum performance (which, after all, is the *raison d'etre* of HPC clusters).

Debugging and monitoring

Logging, monitoring, profiling, and debugging distributed systems, as discussed in *Chapter 7, Testing and Debugging Distributed Applications*, even today is not an easy task, especially when using languages other than C, C++, and Fortran. There is not much more to say here other than the fact that there is an important vacuum to be filled.

Most medium-to-large teams end up developing their own custom solutions based on log aggregators such as Sentry (`https://getsentry.com`) and monitoring solutions such as Ganglia (`http://ganglia.sourceforge.net`).

What would be nice to have are the equivalent of I/O monitoring tools such as Darshan (`http://www.mcs.anl.gov/research/projects/darshan/`) and distributed profilers such as Allinea MAP (`http://www.allinea.com/products/map`) for Python distributed applications.

Where to go next

Building small- to medium-sized distributed applications in Python, as we saw, is not particularly difficult. Once a distributed system grows to a larger size, the design and development effort needed tends to grow as well in a super-linear fashion.

In these cases, a more solid foundation on the theory of distributed systems becomes necessary. There are a number of resources available both online and offline. Most big universities give courses on this subject, and a number of them are freely available online.

One good example is the ETH course on Principles of Distributed Computing (`http://dcg.ethz.ch/lectures/podc_allstars/index.html`), which covers a number of fundamentals, including synchronization, consensus, and eventual consistency (including the famous CAP theorem).

Having said that, beginners should not feel discouraged. The gain in performance that even a few lines of code in a simple framework, such as Python-RQ, can give to our code is just astounding!

Index

A

B

C

Cray systems 108
CUDA 5
Cython 147

D

Darshan
  reference link 150
data trains 146
DDT 132
debugging
  about 150
  defining 128, 129
Directed Acyclic Graph
        Manager (DAGMan) 120
distributed applications
  debugging 132
distributed computing 4-6
Distributed Resource Management
        Application API (DRMAA) 111
distributed system developers
  challenges 132
Docker
  reference link 134

E

EC2 instance
  creating 90-98
Eucalyptus
  about 149
  reference link 104
event-driven programming 14
event loop 3

F

flower
  reference link 66

G

Ganglia
  reference link 150
Global Interpreter Lock (GIL) 36
Graphics Processing Unit (GPU) 2
Grid Engine 109
Gustafson's law 11, 146

H

High Performance Computing (HPC) 107
homebrew
  reference link 51
HPC cluster
  defining 107-109
HPC world
  and cloud 148-150
HTCondor
  about 109, 140
  used, for running Python job 111-122
HyperThreading 54

I

Intel VTune 132
iteration protocol 16

J

job file 112
job schedulers
  about 109
  defining 109-111
Jython 36

L

line_profile 132
LoadLeveler 109
Local Area Network (LAN) 1
logging strategy 141, 142
LSF 109
Luigi
  reference link 148

M

manual, HTCondor
  URL 111
mixed paradigm 12
monitoring process 150
Moore's law 145
multimachine environment
  establishing 47-49

CPSIA information can be obtained
at www.ICGtesting.com
Printed in the USA
FSOW03n0504291016
26689FS